Origami
NINJAS
and other paper sorcery
Colour edition

Models, diagrams and illustrations
by Paul Hanson

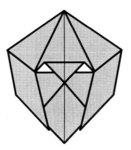

sorceryoforigami.co.uk

Thanks to proofreaders:

Clare Chamberlain
Kathy Knapp
Françoise B Halvorsen
John Allen

Index

Introduction

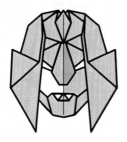

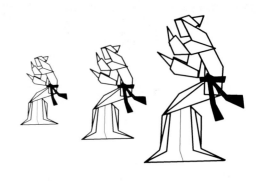

This book would not have been possible without the help and influence of others.

A number of people in the London origami group, have helped me understand how to create new origami models, and improve my work. And just as importantly through this group, I have had lots of laughs along the way.

The London group would not have existed without the British Origami Society who continue to inspire and support folders everywhere. For more information see <Britishorigami.info>.

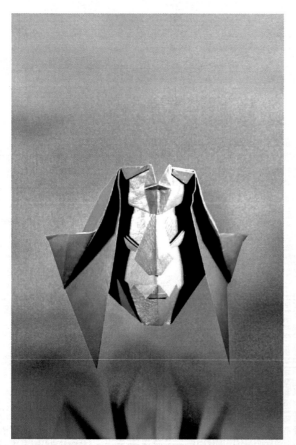

Elserealm superhero mask

About some of the models

Faces
There are a number of faces in the book ranging from demons to jesters. My aim was to create origami faces which are dynamic. One special quality I have experienced in origami is improvisation. It is quite different from drawing with a pencil where anything is possible (or perhaps limited by your own technical ability), the fact that the paper is restrictive itself enables improvisation. Folding with an open mind created all of these faces, and although I may have started with an intention, I was not dissuaded from pursuing other ideas as they appeared in the paper.

Bird base dragon
There are many traditional models in origami - but no dragon. If there had been a traditional origami dragon, this is my idea of what it would look like.

If pigs might flap
This was in response to a challenge set at one of the London origami group meetings to create something that flaps, which is not a bird. It just had to be done! This is a flapping action model.

Syringe and Vampira
The Syringe and Vampira were originally created for a hospital themed charity event. The syringe will appear to withdraw blood or inject a substance, when the plunger is moved. Vampira has previously been published in 'World's Best Origami' by Nick Robinson.

Coffee stirrer rest
Halfway through the book, you will find this simple practical fold. If you are working through the book model by model why not reward yourself and relax in your local coffee shop and try this fold. A reaction to my frustration of where to

put my stirrer in coffee shops that do not provide a saucer. Now you can stir your coffee more than once and not make a mess on the table.

Martial arts figure

Created for a martial arts club display, the model is intended to depict the old joke about a black belt in origami. This model started my adult interest in origami and was inspired by one of Robert Harbin's books (Origami 3). He had included a skier figure and explained that it was made from a Neal Elias figure base. Robert suggested readers could try creating their own figures from this base. So I gave it a try. Even to this day I am pleased with this model. It owes much to Neal Elias and, as I was later to find out, also Iris Walker (a founder of the British Origami Society) who, I understand, introduced Neal to the figure base when she was experimenting with a technique known as box pleating. This was my first introduction to creating something new and inspired me to try creating other figures.

Origami Ninjas, Cool werewolf

My aim with human figures is to include a representation of human anatomy, including muscle structure, which is rarely attempted in origami.

The bird-frog hybrid base is not the most well known of traditional bases, but has been used by a few origami creators for animals and flat human figures. I believe Yoshihide Momotani was the first origami creator who published the use of this base for human figures in 'Origami of taste'. This base is interesting as the proportions are very close to being correct for human figures. Inspired by this work, I thought this base could be taken further, including a realistic representation of human anatomy by sculpting the base into a 3D form to represent the chest, arm and leg muscles. My first design using the bird-frog base was the Origami Ninja, created in 2009.

The Cool werewolf model extends this base by a technique known as grafting, which effectively adds additional paper for the head, something I picked up from Robert Lang's 'Origami Design Secrets'.

The Dark wizard

One of my favourite models - I remember the moment the long hood came into being, it sort of fell into place. I have been told the model is scary!

Perhaps one for Halloween; and don't turn out the light.

Weapons

There are a few weapons. The katana sword, nunchukas and throwing star were necessary accessories for the Ninja. The throwing star is a traditional model I felt had to be included for completeness.

The model I designed for the 'RED 2' film is also included. It plays a vital role in setting up one of the lead characters and I feel actually defines this character very clearly. I was impressed by the scriptwriter's choice to use origami in this respect. It was a fun project to be involved in.

I hope this book will inspire you to create your own sorcery.

The Dark wizard

Folding advice

The following folding tips are recommended to make the best use of this book.

1. Learn the meaning of the symbols shown on the following page, these will be your guide. Folds are represented by a series of dotted and /or dashed lines. The direction of the fold by an arrow style.

2. Unless otherwise stated, when folding, make your creases sharp - this will help you create more accurate models.

3. Do not expect your first attempt of folding a model to be perfect. The first time you fold a model, will allow you to learn the folds and recognise their importance in the models sequence the next time.

4. Always look at the next step, it will tell you the final position of the fold you are making in the current step.

5. Allow for 'creep' in some cases. Some models involve folding the paper over in one direction two or more times. In such cases the paper will creep closer to the centre of the folds and overlap or cause bucking. To avoid this in such cases, leave a slight gap between the fold and the meeting line or edge. A symbol identifies when this is recommended in the diagrams.

6. Some models in this book have a few final steps which involve folding to create the anatomy of a human figure - in most cases these are judgment folds, and are represented with lines showing an estimate of human proportions. You will improve these steps if you have a knowledge of anatomy. See the section in the book 'Creating dynamic anatomy with origami' on page 131.

How to fold diagonals accurately

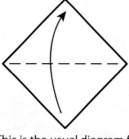

This is the usual diagram for a diagonal fold

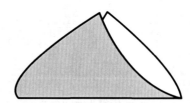

1. Line up points of paper accurately.

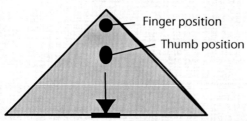

2. Hold points in place with finger and thumb, then with the other hand draw a finger straight down vertically and make small crease at bottom.

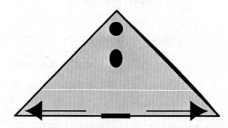

3. Now without moving your finger and thumb, use the other hand to crease to the right and then to the left in the direction of the arrows.

Key to symbols

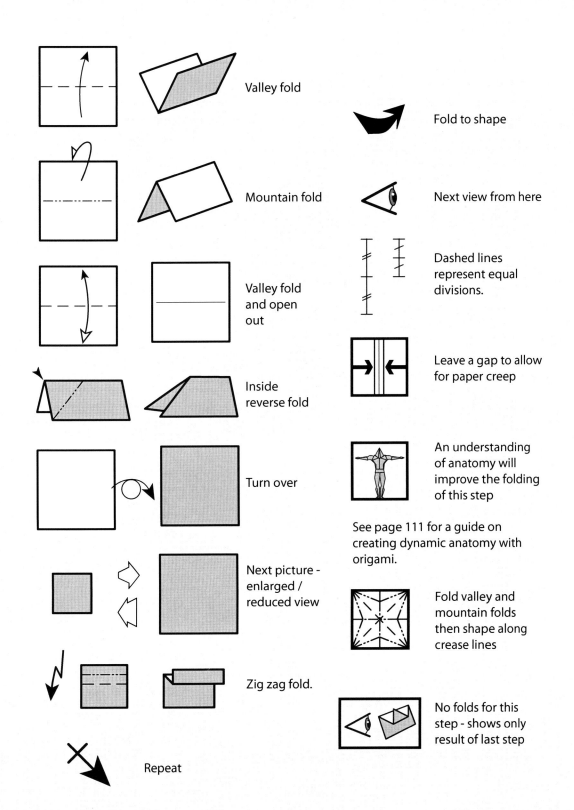

Valley fold

Mountain fold

Valley fold and open out

Inside reverse fold

Turn over

Next picture - enlarged / reduced view

Zig zag fold.

Repeat

Fold to shape

Next view from here

Dashed lines represent equal divisions.

Leave a gap to allow for paper creep

An understanding of anatomy will improve the folding of this step

See page 111 for a guide on creating dynamic anatomy with origami.

Fold valley and mountain folds then shape along crease lines

No folds for this step - shows only result of last step

Model Index

• simple model
• • intermediate model
• • • high intermediate model

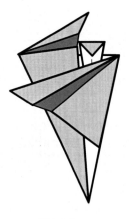

Vampira
• (p12)

Bird base dragon
• • (p15)

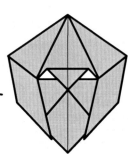

Face of the ninja
• (p18)

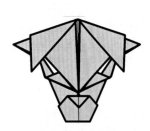

Face of the demon
• • (p21)

Master demon face
• • (p24)

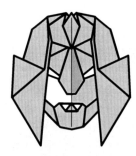

Elserealm superhero
mask
• • (p25)

Demon jester
• • • (p29)

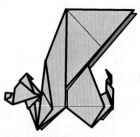

If pigs might flap
• • (p35)

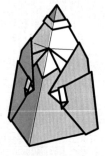

Father Christmas
• • (p42)

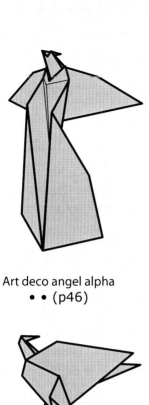

Art deco angel alpha
• • (p46)

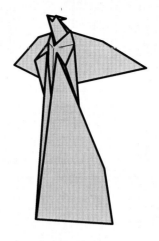

Art deco angel beta
• • (p50)

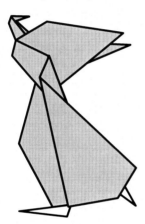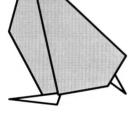

Ice skating angel
• • (p52)

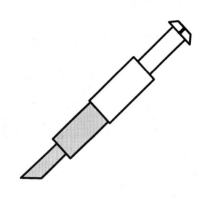

Syringe
• • (p58)

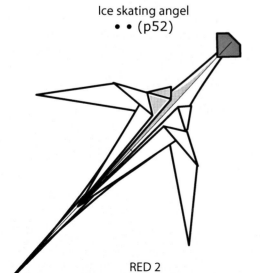

RED 2
Sci weapon
• • • (p60)

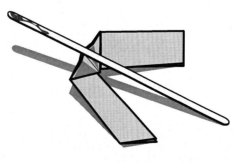

Coffee shop stirrer stand
• (p65)

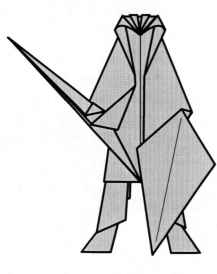

Knight
• • (p67)

Dark wizard
• • (p71)

Martial arts figure
• • • (p74)

Cool werewolf
• • • (p78)

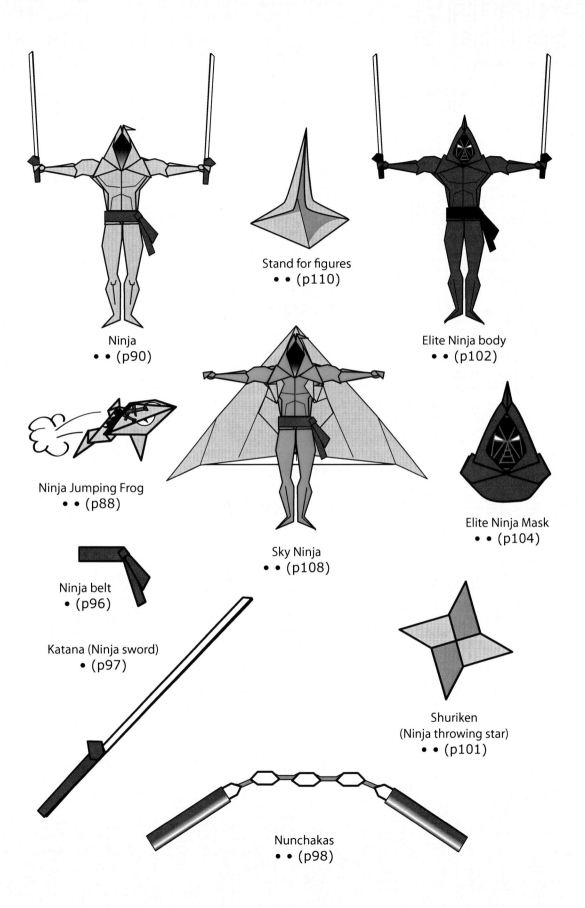

Ninja
• • (p90)

Stand for figures
• • (p110)

Elite Ninja body
• • (p102)

Ninja Jumping Frog
• • (p88)

Sky Ninja
• • (p108)

Elite Ninja Mask
• • (p104)

Ninja belt
• (p96)

Katana (Ninja sword)
• (p97)

Shuriken
(Ninja throwing star)
• • (p101)

Nunchakas
• • (p98)

Vampira

Vampira

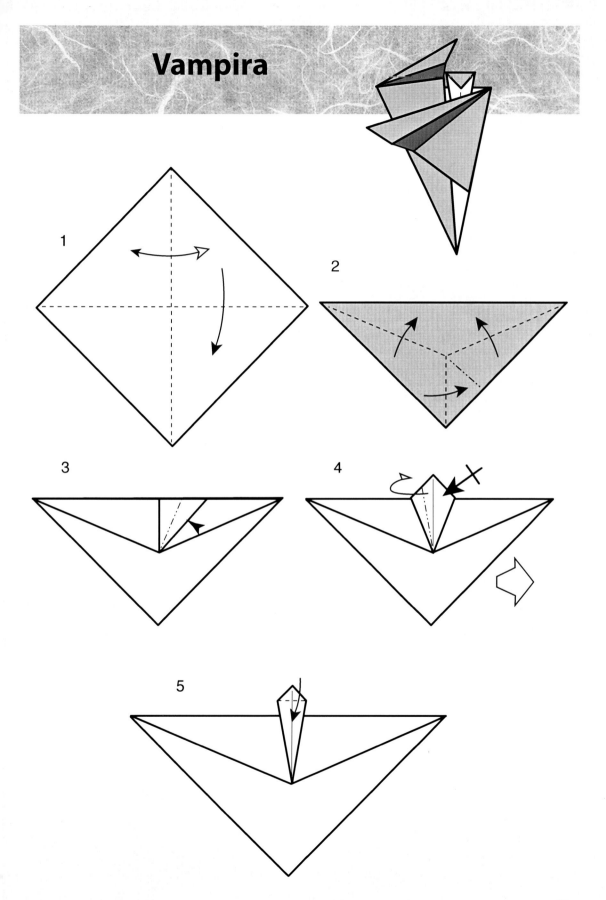

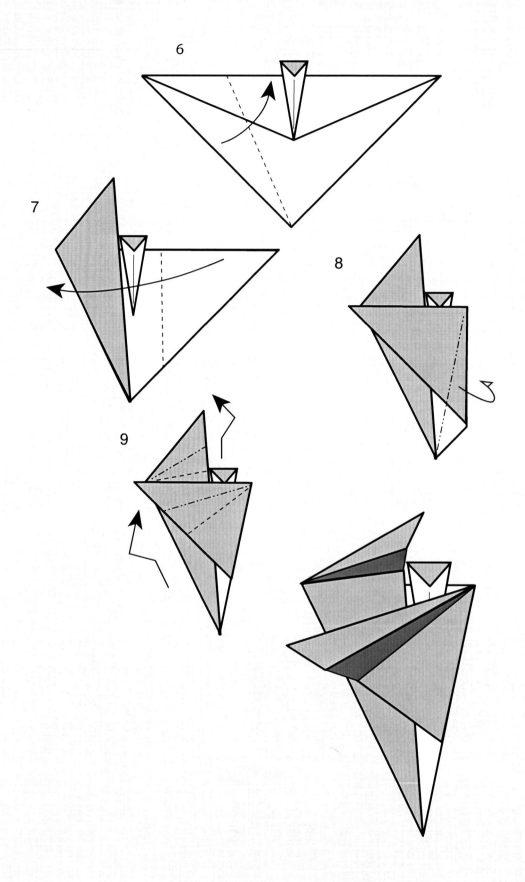

Bird base dragon

Bird base dragon

1

2

3

4

5

6

7

8

9

10

16

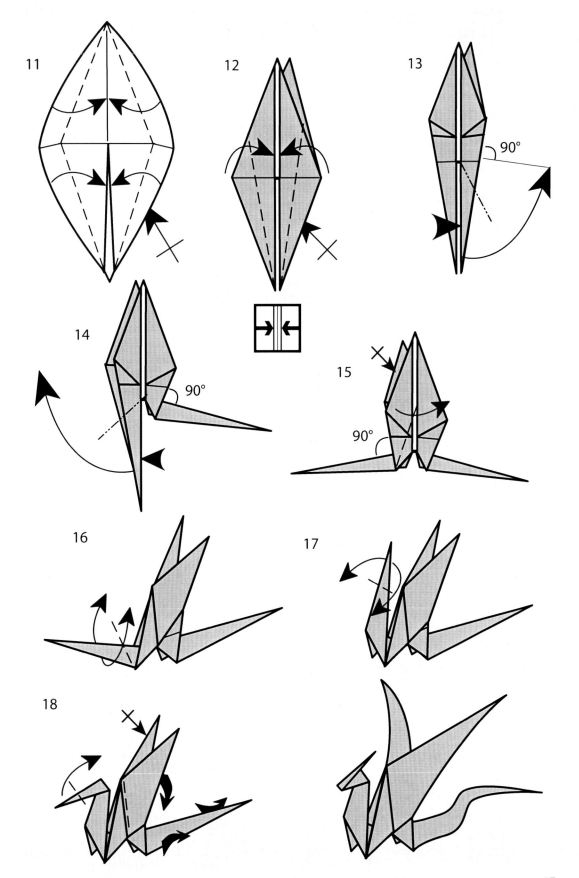

Face of the ninja

Face of the ninja

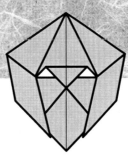

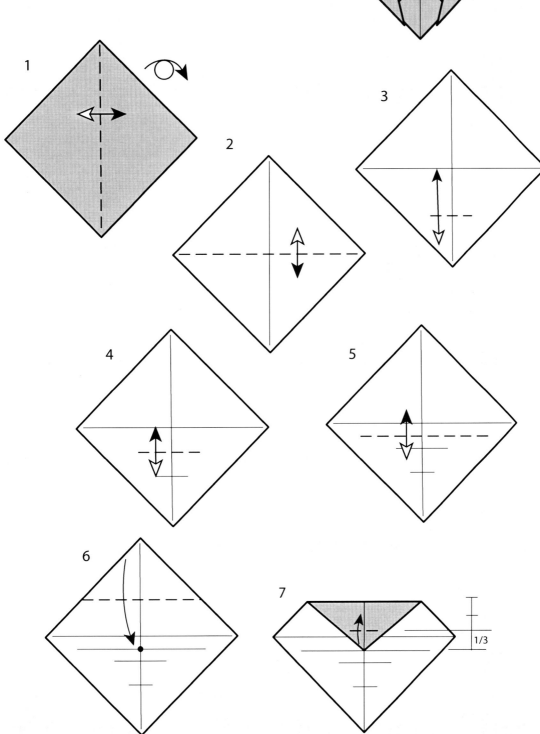

1

2

3

4

5

6

7

1/3

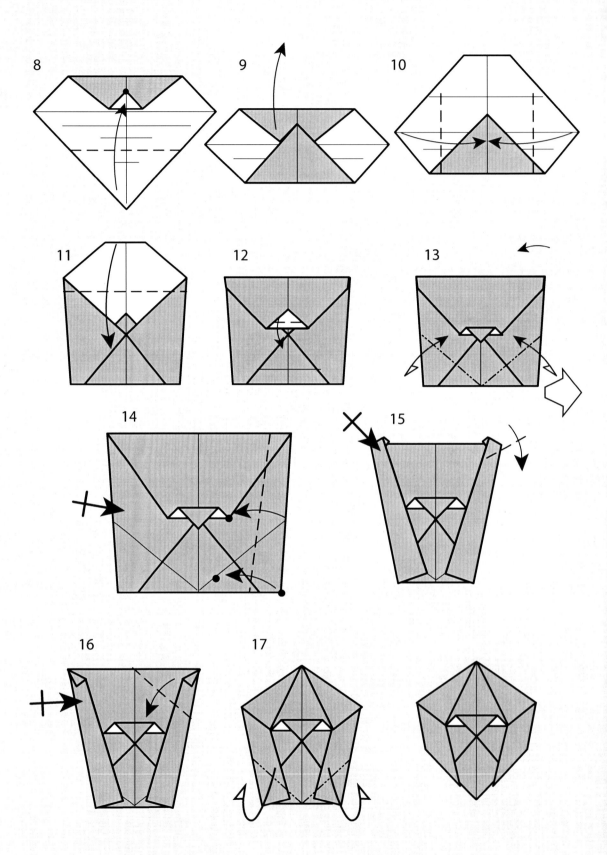

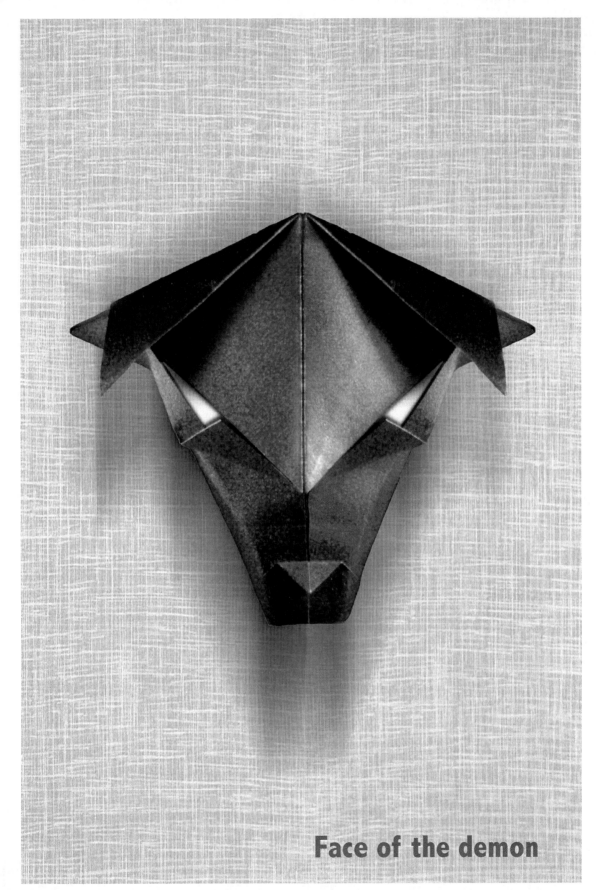

Face of the demon

Face of the demon

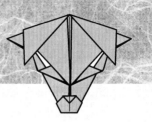

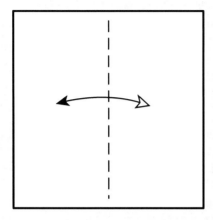

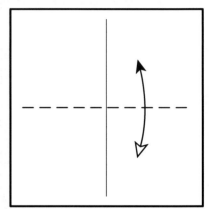

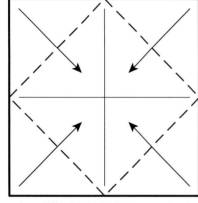

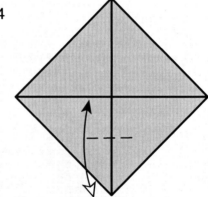

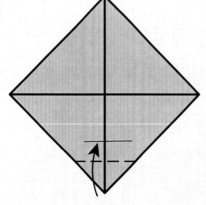

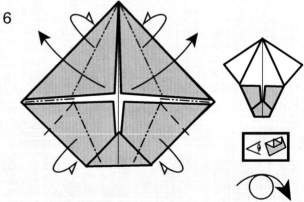

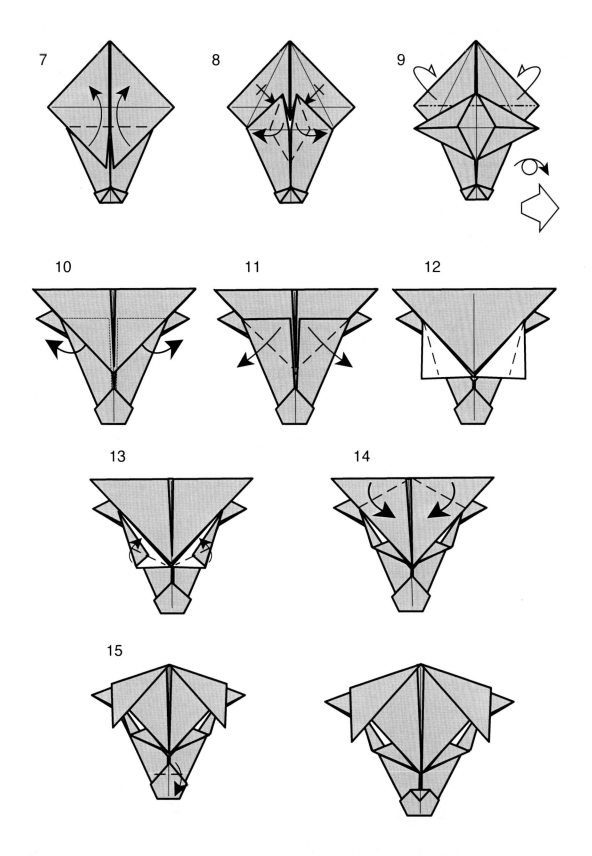

23

Master demon face

Add the following steps to the 'Face of the demon' model.

15a

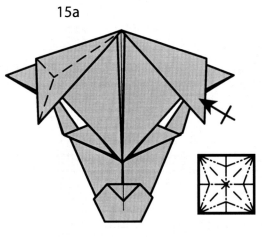

16a

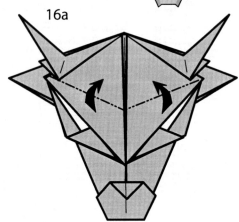

17a

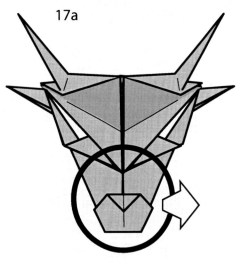

18a

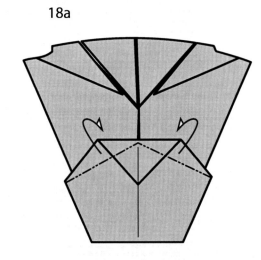

19a

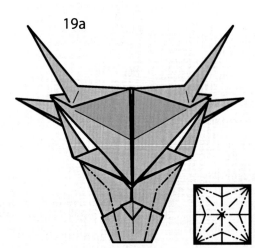

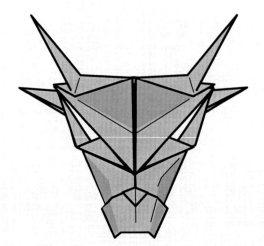

Elserealm superhero mask

Elserealm superhero mask

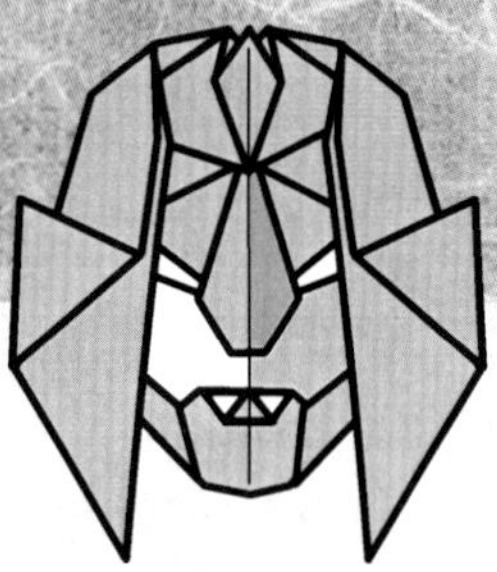

1

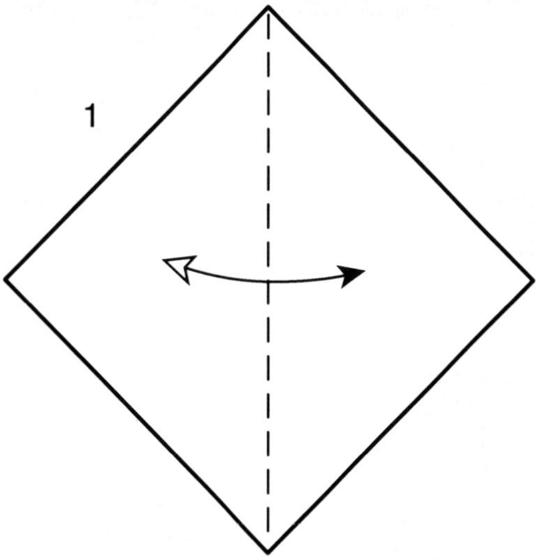

2

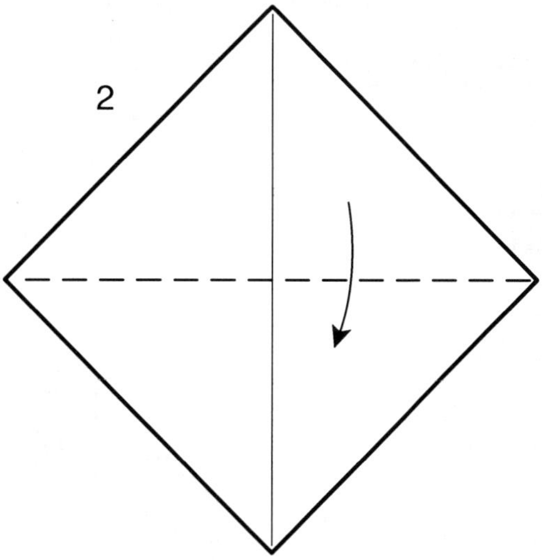

3

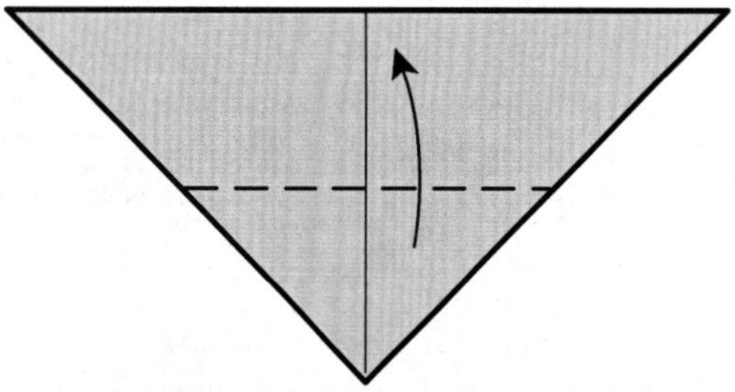

4

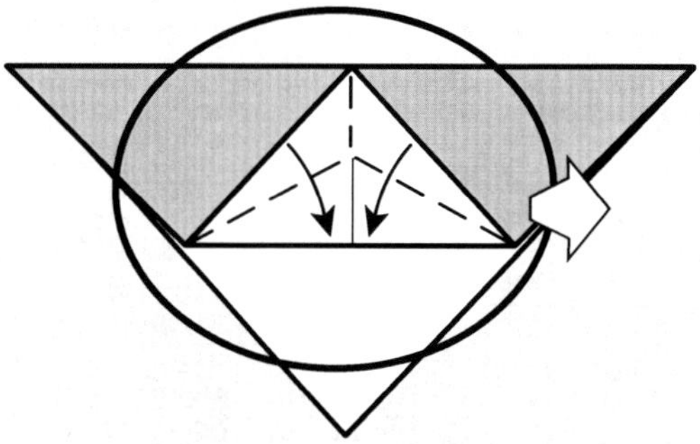

5

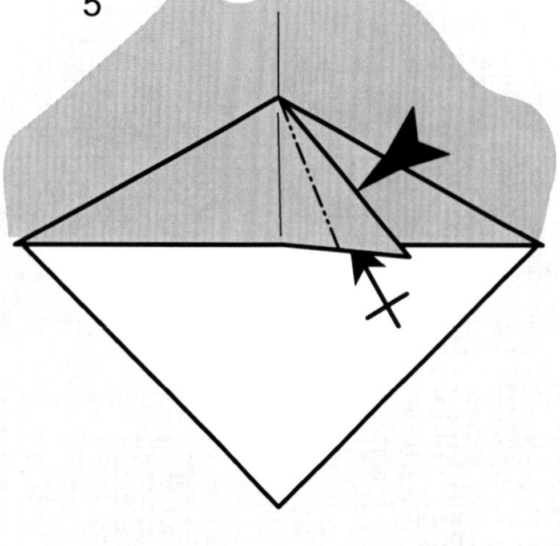

6

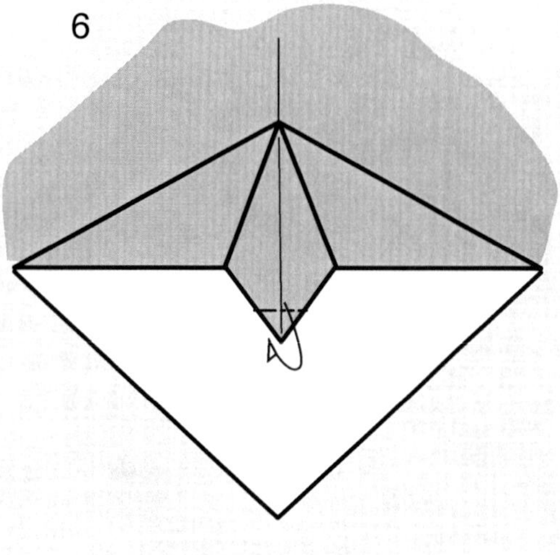

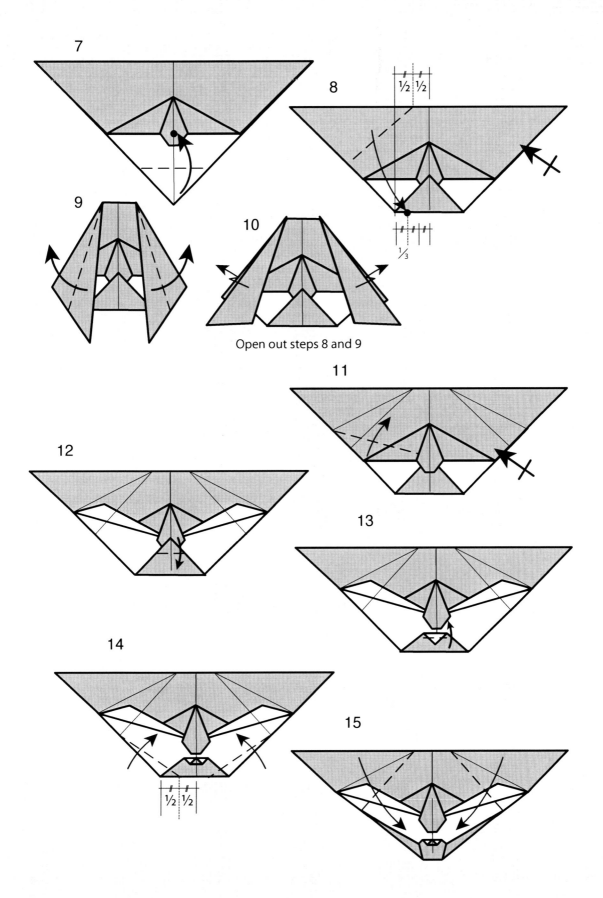

Open out steps 8 and 9

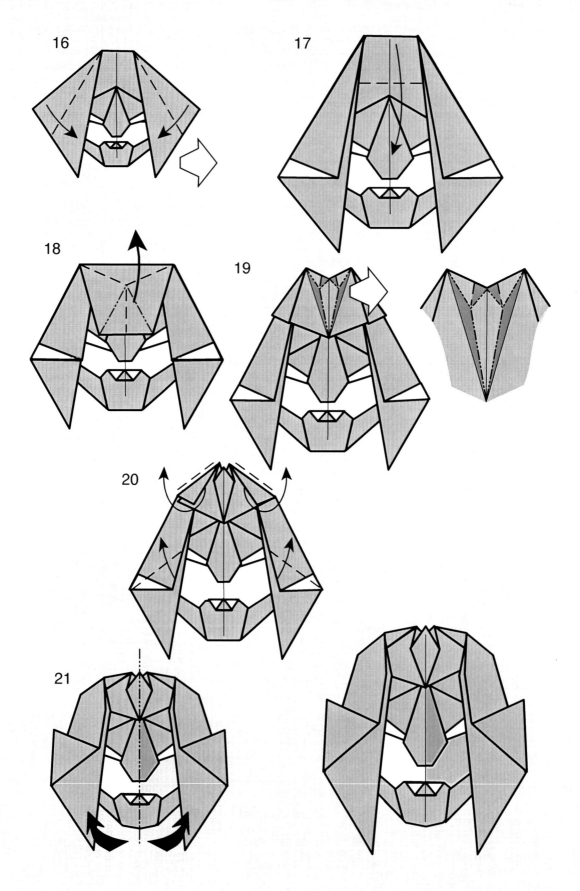

Demon jester

Demon jester

1

2

3

4

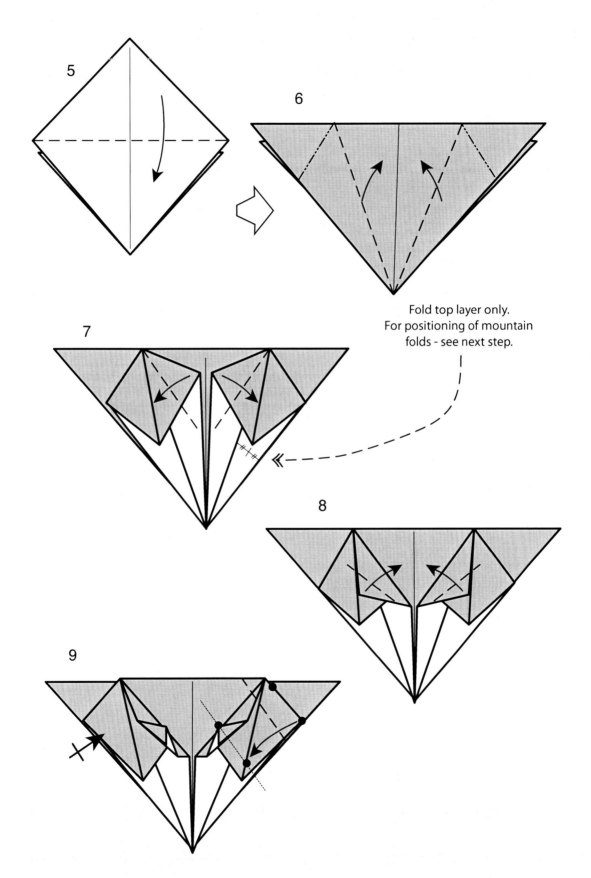

5

6

Fold top layer only.
For positioning of mountain
folds - see next step.

7

8

9

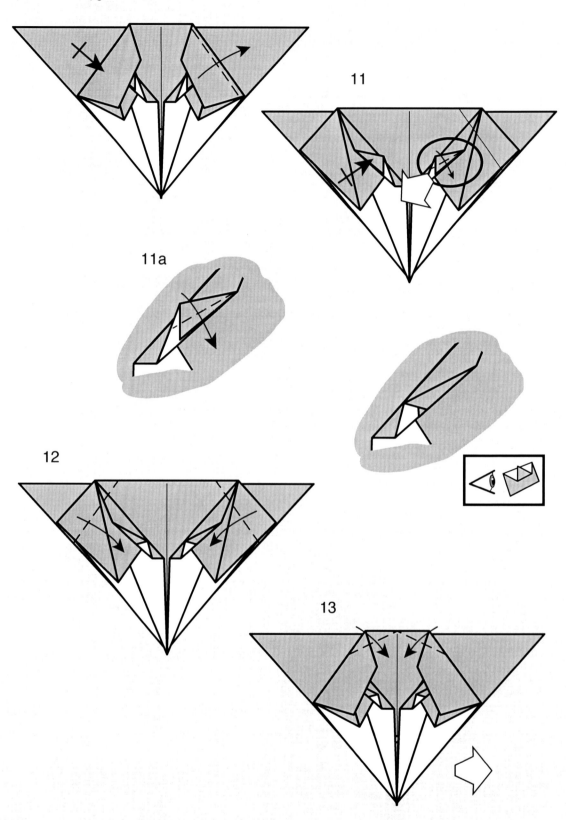

10

11

11a

12

13

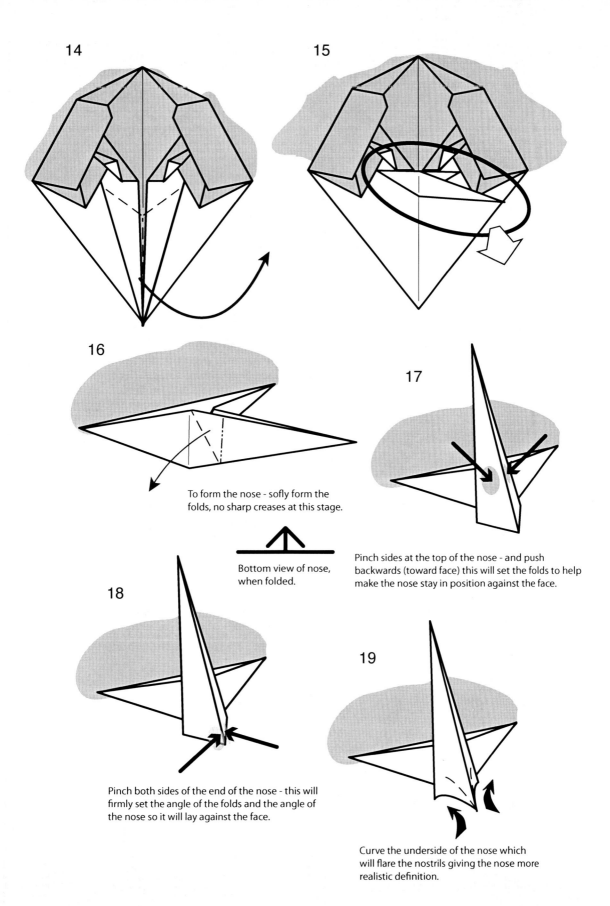

14

15

16

To form the nose - sofly form the folds, no sharp creases at this stage.

Bottom view of nose, when folded.

17

Pinch sides at the top of the nose - and push backwards (toward face) this will set the folds to help make the nose stay in position against the face.

18

Pinch both sides of the end of the nose - this will firmly set the angle of the folds and the angle of the nose so it will lay against the face.

19

Curve the underside of the nose which will flare the nostrils giving the nose more realistic definition.

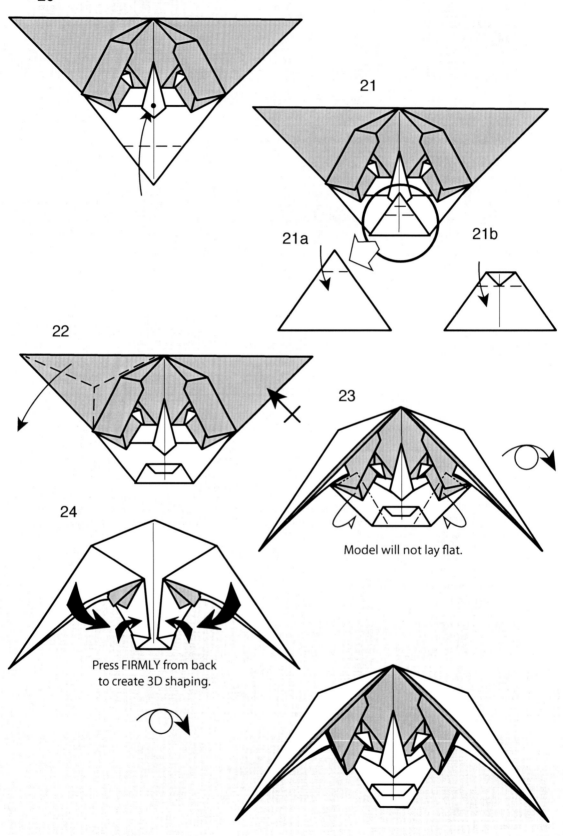

20

21

21a

21b

22

23

Model will not lay flat.

24

Press FIRMLY from back
to create 3D shaping.

If pigs might flap

If pigs might flap

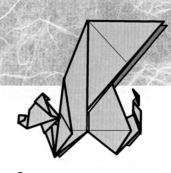

1

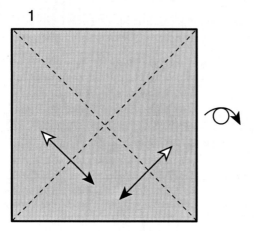

2

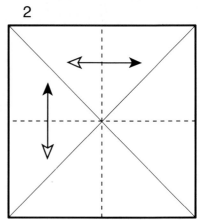

3

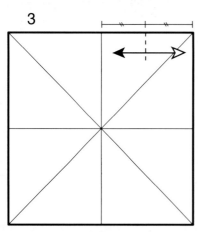

4

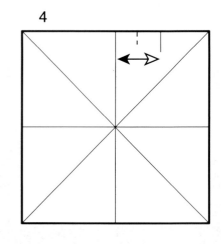

5

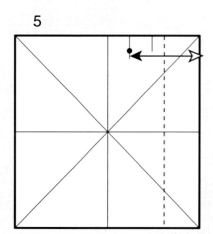

6

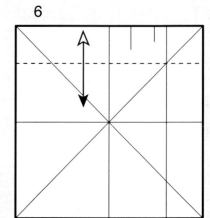

7

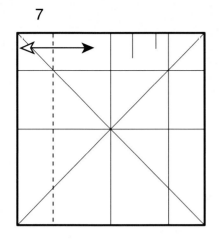

8

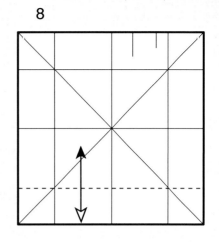

9

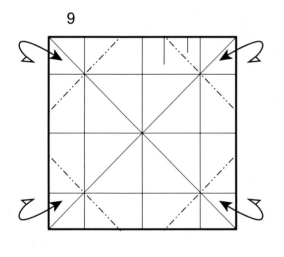

10

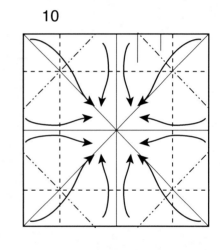

11

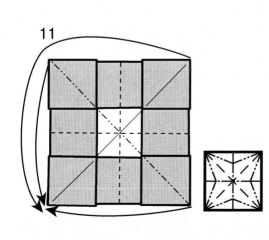

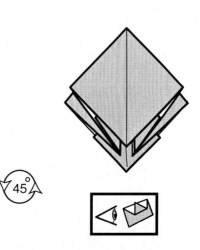

45°

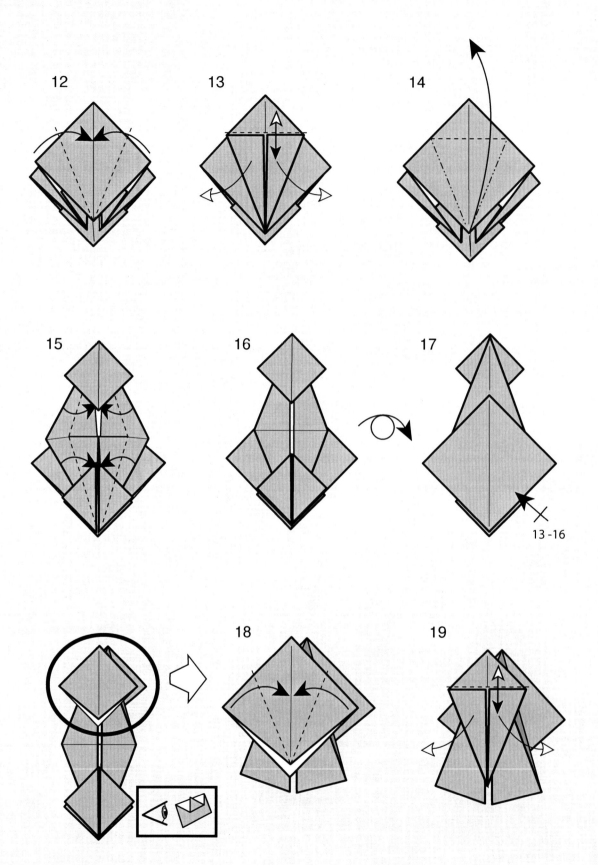

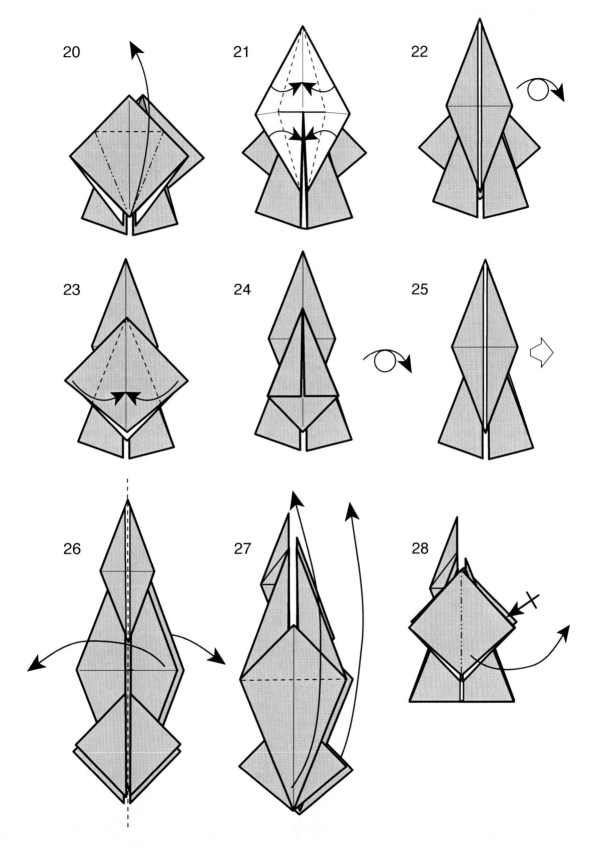

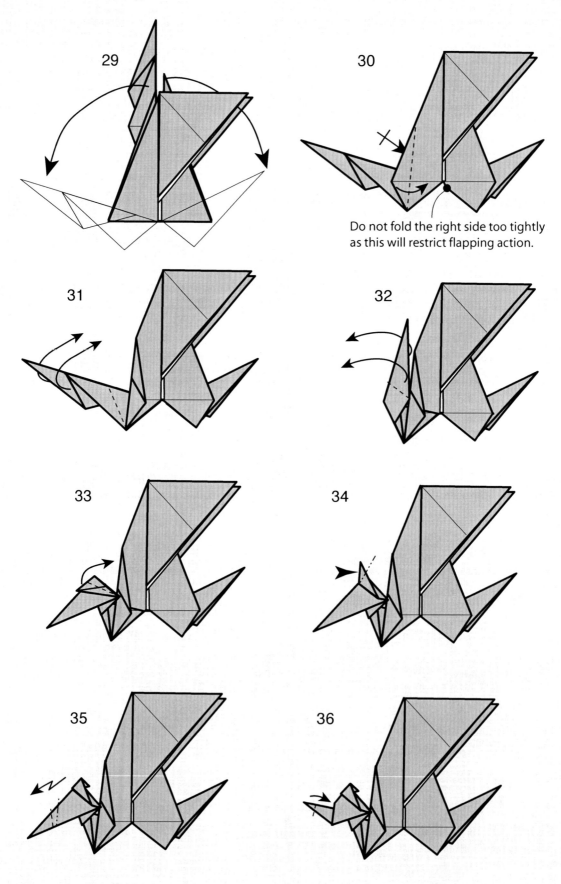

29

30

Do not fold the right side too tightly
as this will restrict flapping action.

31

32

33

34

35

36

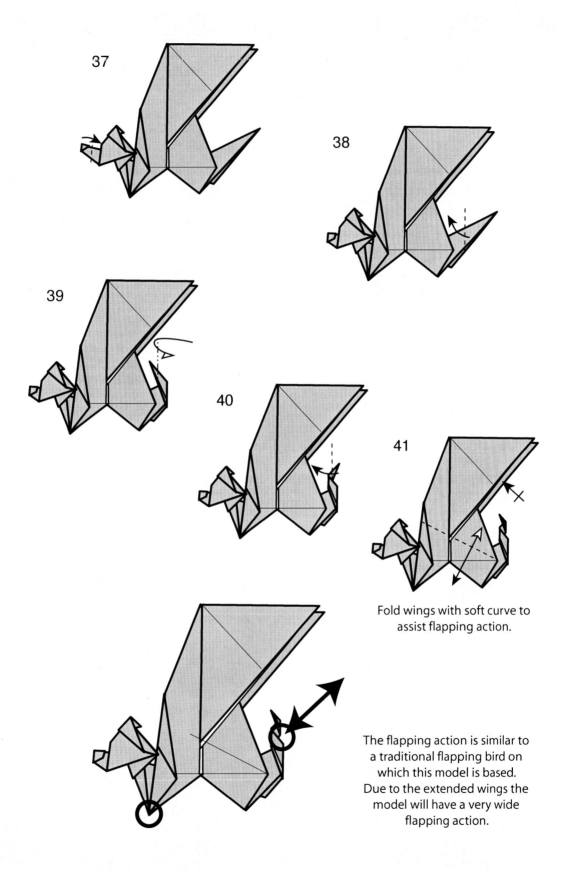

37

38

39

40

41

Fold wings with soft curve to assist flapping action.

The flapping action is similar to a traditional flapping bird on which this model is based. Due to the extended wings the model will have a very wide flapping action.

Father Christmas

Father Christmas

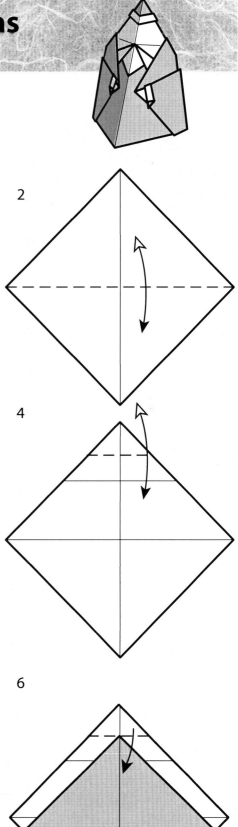

1

2

3

4

5

6

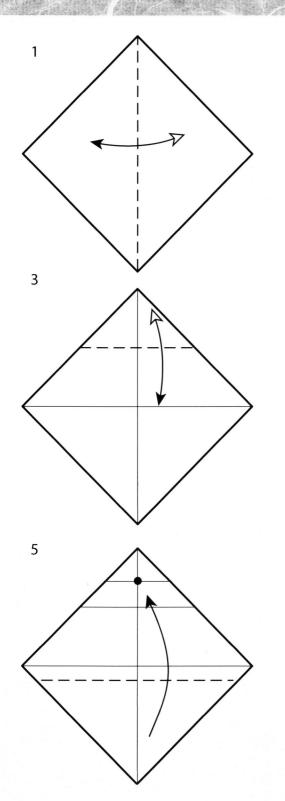

7

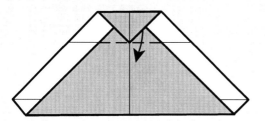

8

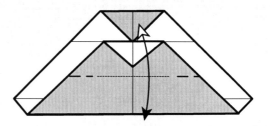

9

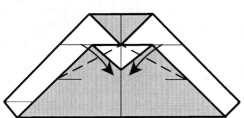

10

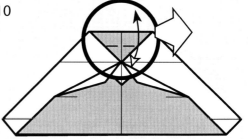

11

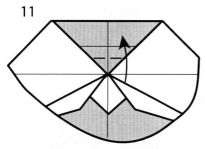

12

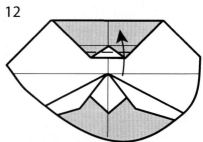

13

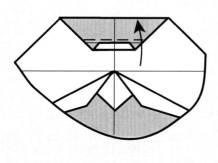

15

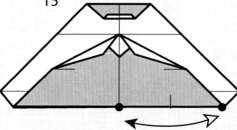

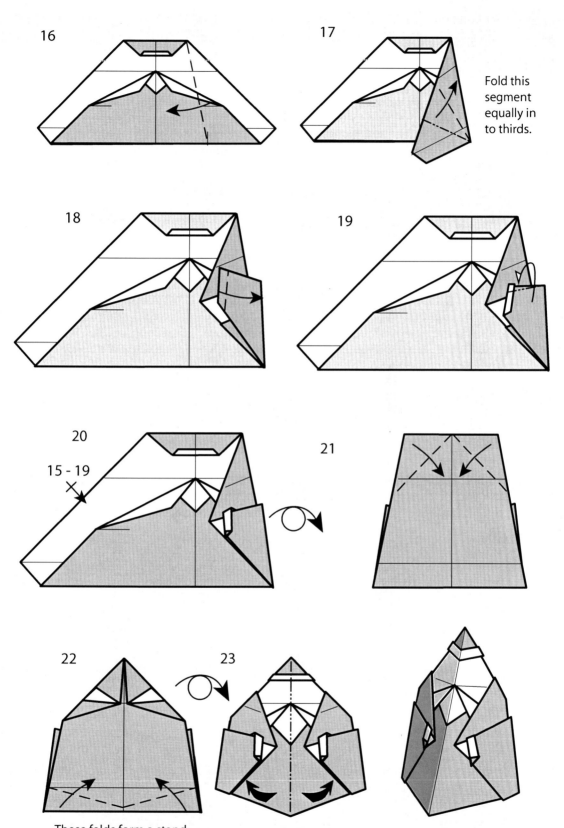

16

17

Fold this segment equally in to thirds.

18

19

20

15 - 19

21

22

These folds form a stand.

23

Art deco angels

Art deco angel alpha

1

2

3

4

5

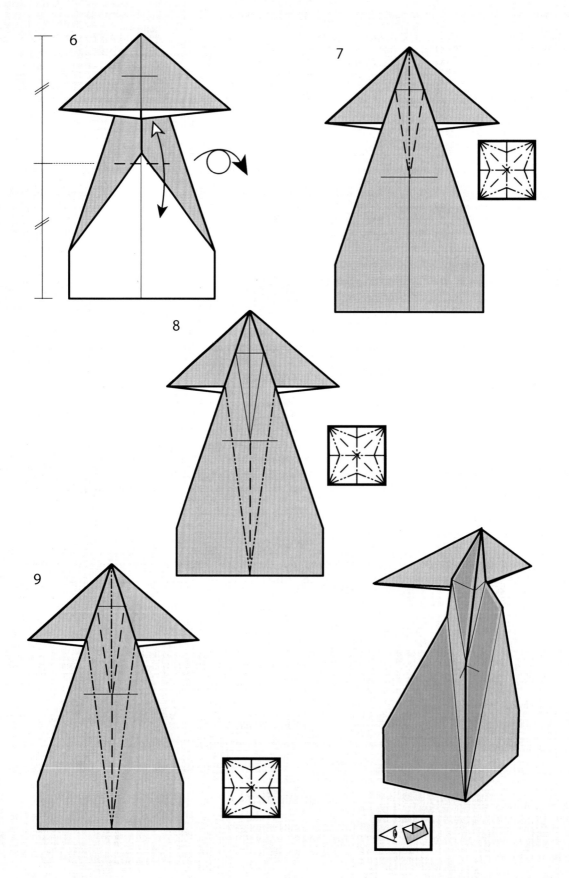

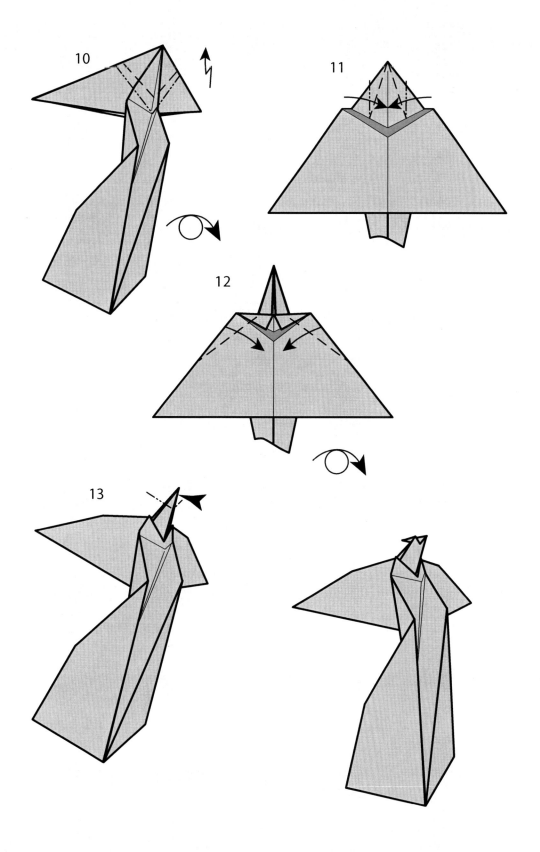

Art deco angel beta

This variation of the Art Deco Angel is slightly harder than the
Alpha version and adds a different expression to the arms.

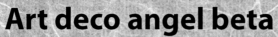

Fold up to step 6 of Art Deco Angel Alpha.

7

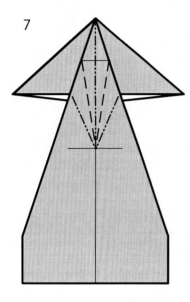

8a

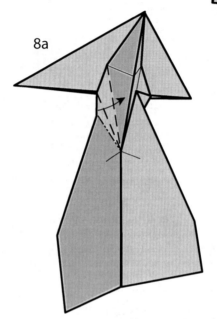

8

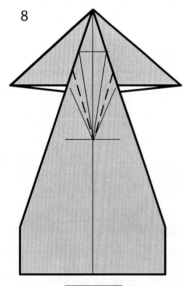

9

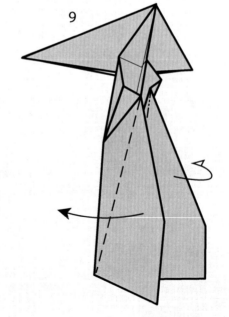

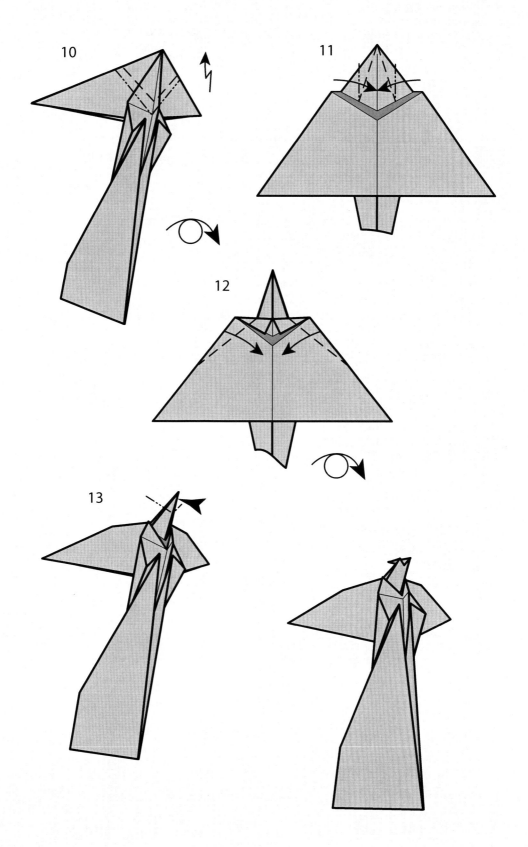

Ice skating angel

Ice skating angel

1

2

3

4

5

6

7

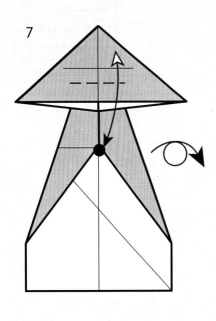

8

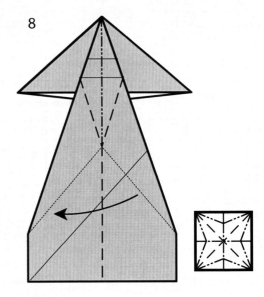

9

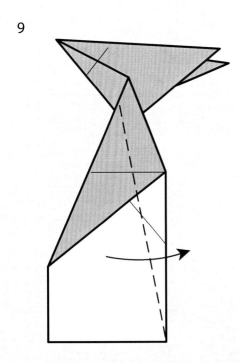

10

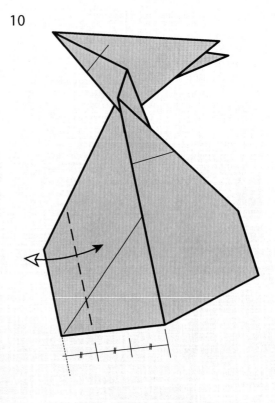

11

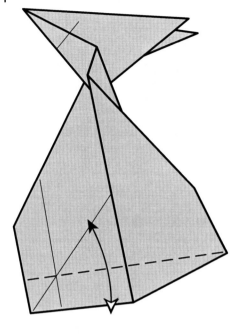

12

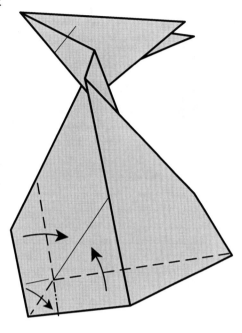

13

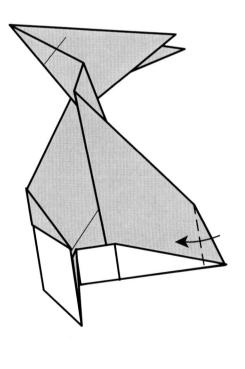

14

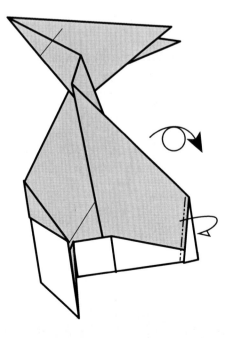

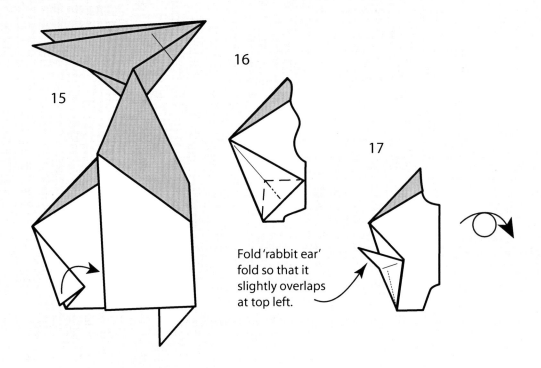

15

16

17

Fold 'rabbit ear'
fold so that it
slightly overlaps
at top left.

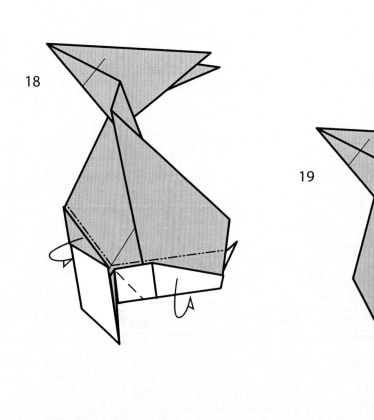

18

19

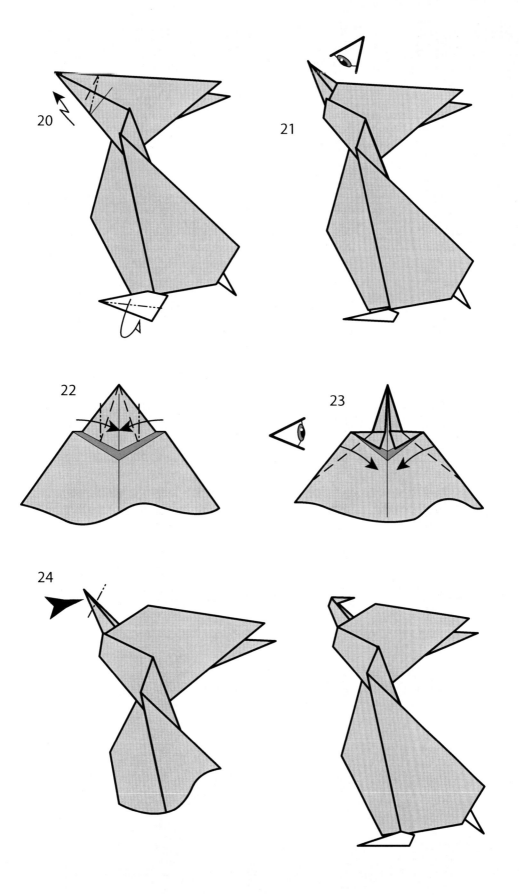

20

21

22

23

24

Syringe

Two piece figure

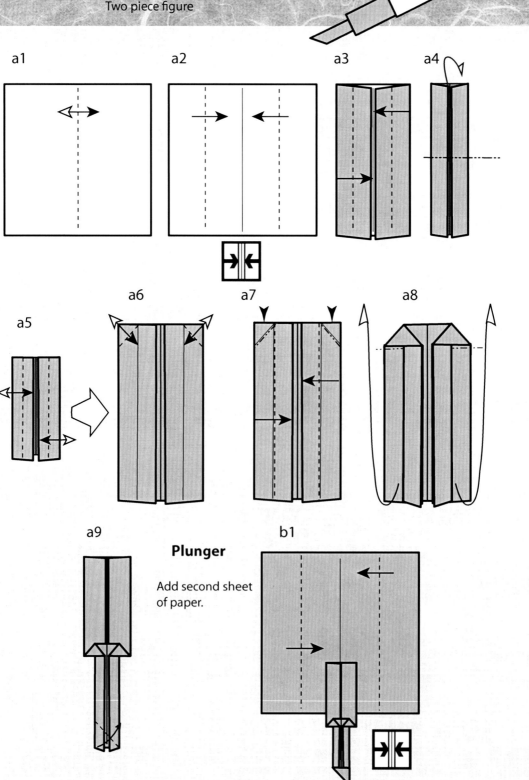

a1

a2

a3

a4

a5

a6

a7

a8

a9

Plunger

Add second sheet of paper.

b1

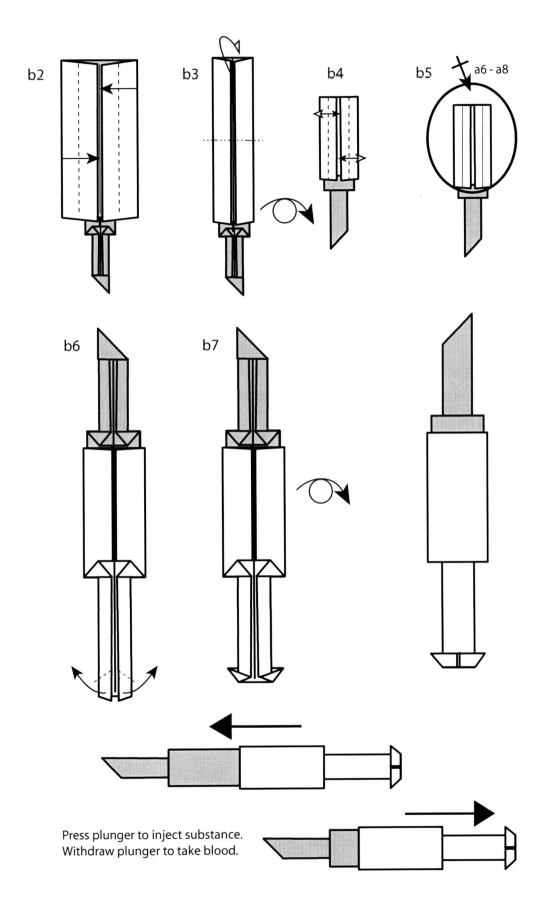

b2

b3

b4

b5   a6 - a8

b6

b7

Press plunger to inject substance.
Withdraw plunger to take blood.

THE BEST NEVER REST

BRUCE **WILLIS** JOHN **MALKOVICH** MARY-LOUISE **PARKER** CATHERINE **ZETA-JONES** BYUNG HUN **LEE** with ANTHONY **HOPKINS** and HELEN **MIRREN**

RED 2

SUMMIT ENTERTAINMENT PRESENTS A A OF BONAVENTURA PICTURES PRODUCTION BRUCE WILLIS JOHN MALKOVICH MARY LOUISE PARKER WITH ANTHONY HOPKINS AND HELEN MIRREN "RED 2"
CATHERINE ZETA-JONES BYUNG HUN LEE BRIAN COX NEAL McDONOUGH CASTING BY DEBORAH AQUILA CSA AND TRICIA WOOD CSA VISUAL EFFECTS SUPERVISOR JAMES MADIGAN MUSIC SUPERVISOR JOHN HOULIHAN
MUSIC COMPOSED AND CONDUCTED BY ALAN SILVESTRI COSTUME DESIGNER BEATRIX ARUNA PASZTOR EDITOR DON ZIMMERMAN A.C.E. PRODUCTION DESIGNER JIM CLAY DIRECTOR OF PHOTOGRAPHY ENRIQUE CHEDIAK ASC EXECUTIVE PRODUCERS JAKE MYERS DAVID READY
PRODUCED BY LORENZO DI BONAVENTURA MARK VAHRADIAN BASED ON CHARACTERS CREATED BY WARREN ELLIS AND CULLY HAMNER WRITTEN BY JON HOEBER & ERICH HOEBER DIRECTED BY DEAN PARISOT

  SUMMER THIS FILM IS NOT YET RATED

RED 2 Sci Weapon

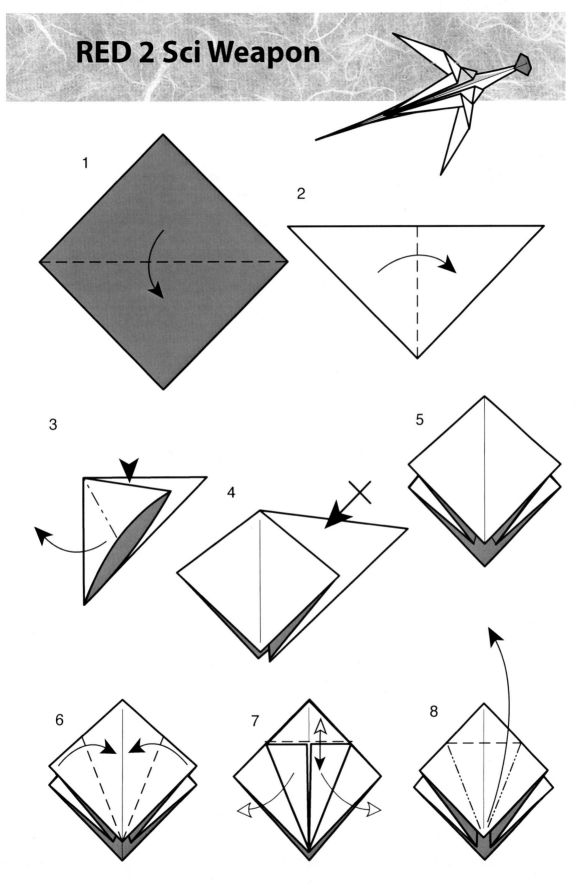

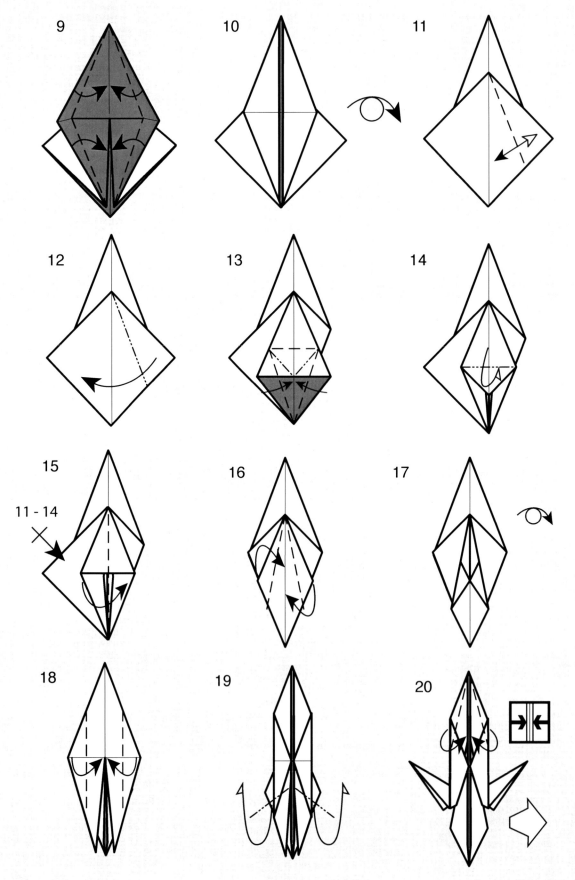

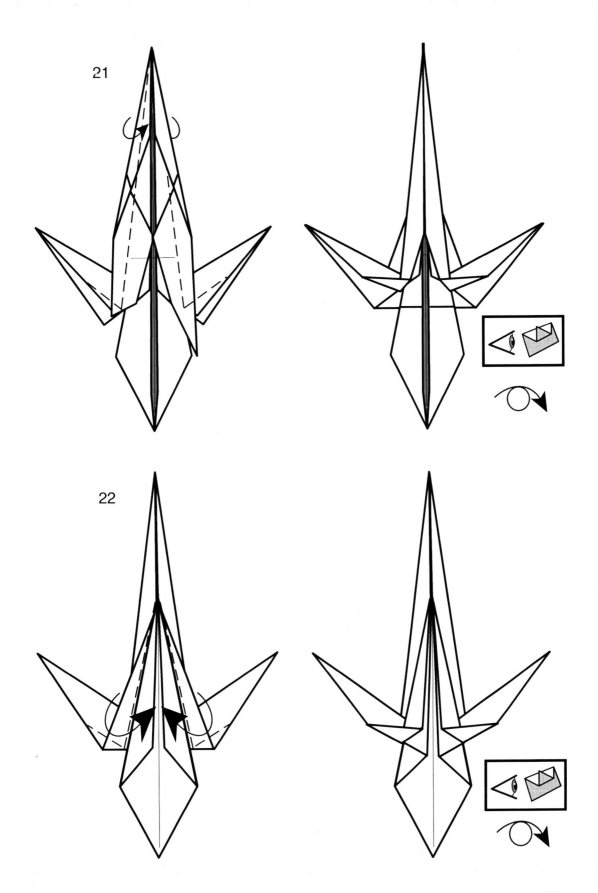

21

22

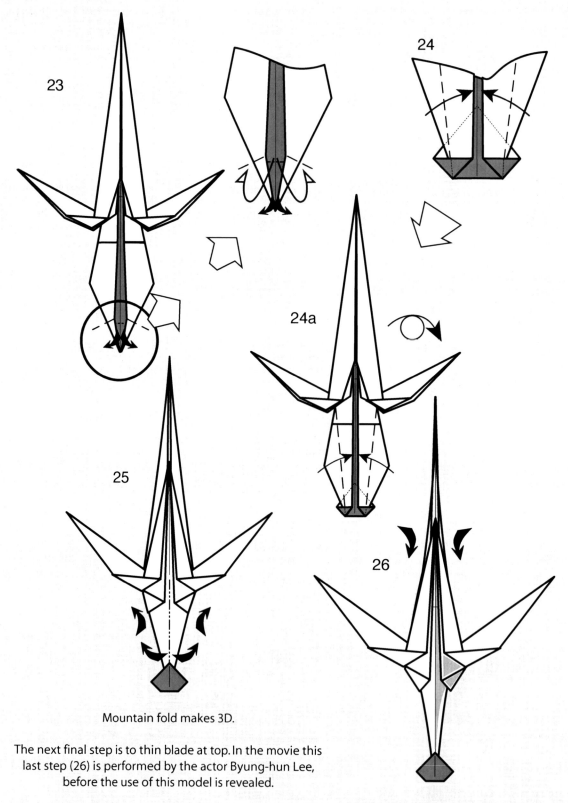

23

24

24a

25

26

Mountain fold makes 3D.

The next final step is to thin blade at top. In the movie this
last step (26) is performed by the actor Byung-hun Lee,
before the use of this model is revealed.

Byung-hun Lee talks *'Red 2, working with
Bruce Willis, and the strength of origami'*
youtu.be/-MPaz3D85w8

Coffee shop stirrer stand

Coffee shop stirrer stand

Any napkin, square or rectangular will be suitable, even if top layer is shorter, as shown in step 1.

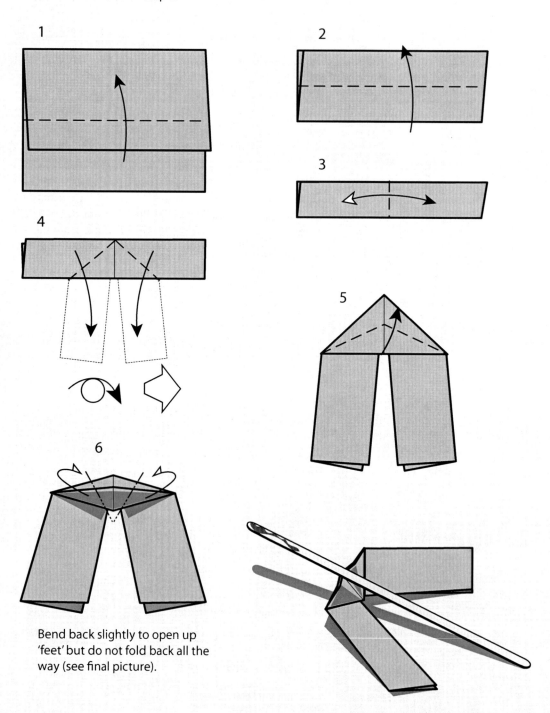

1

2

3

4

5

6

Bend back slightly to open up 'feet' but do not fold back all the way (see final picture).

Knight

Knight

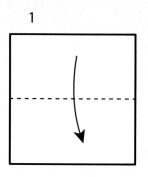

1

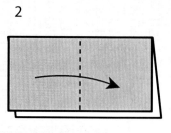

2

3

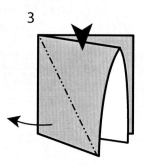

4

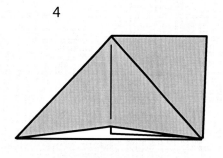

5

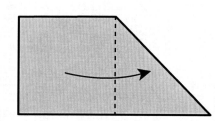

6

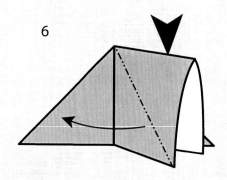

7

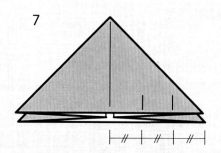

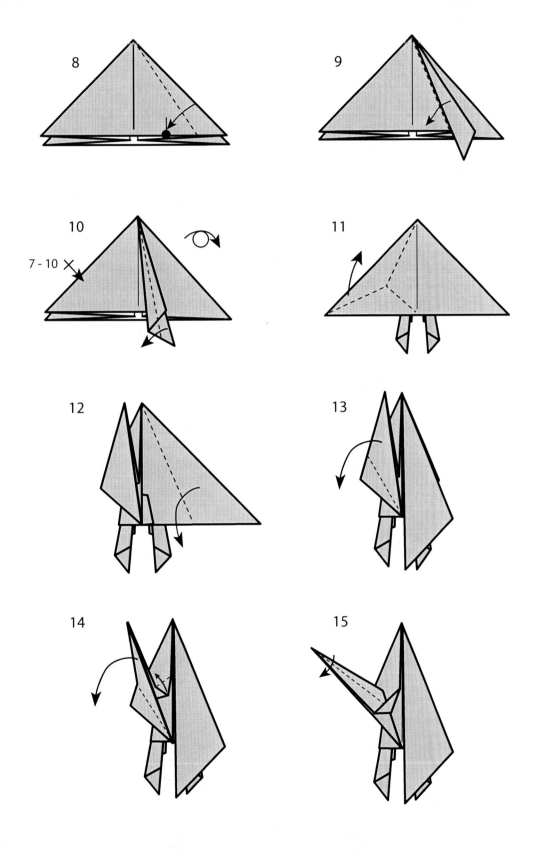

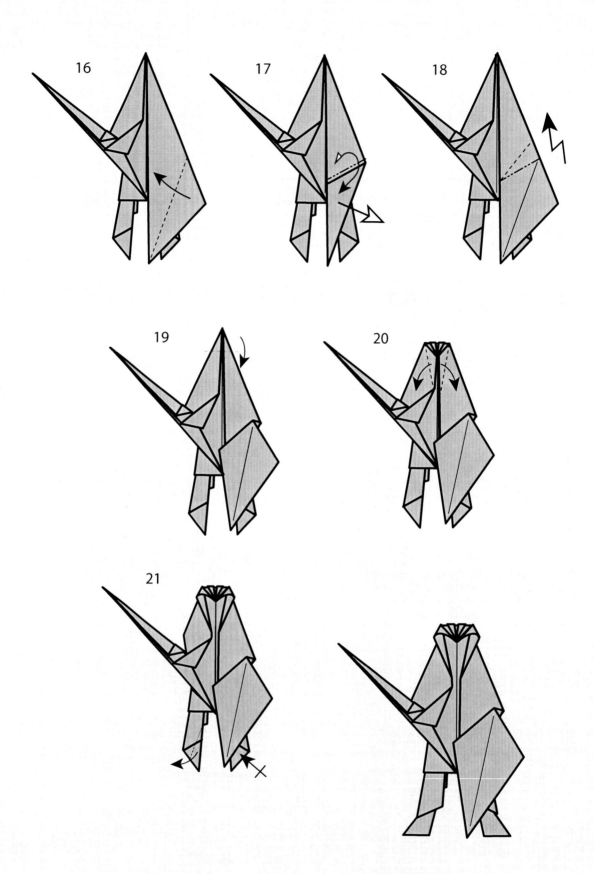

Dark wizard

Dark wizard

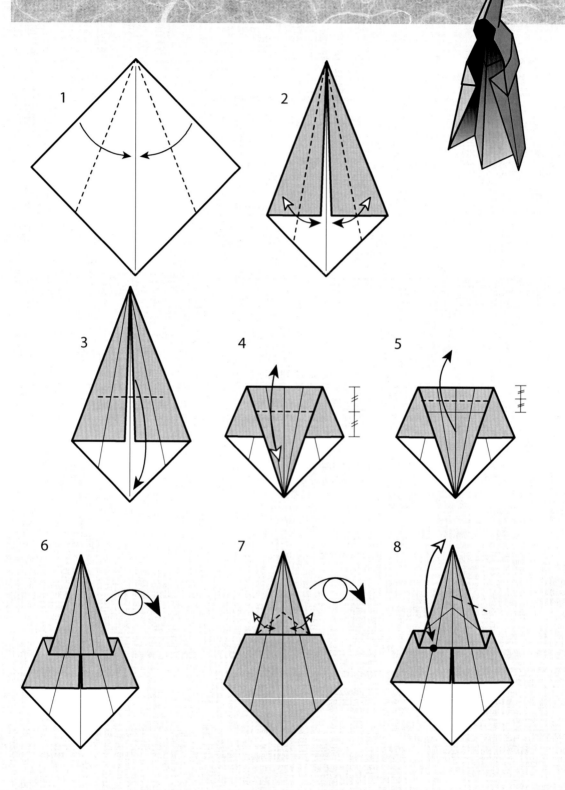

1

2

3

4

5

6

7

8

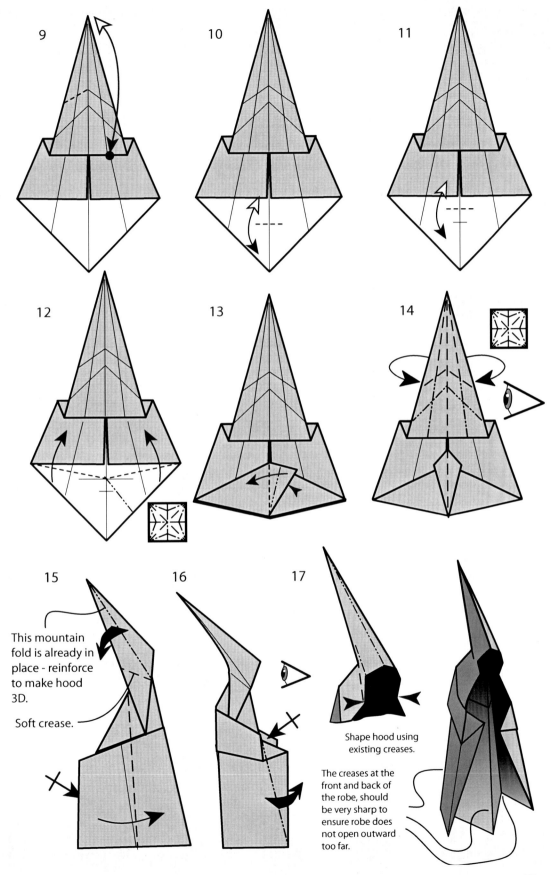

9

10

11

12

13

14

15

This mountain fold is already in place - reinforce to make hood 3D.

Soft crease.

16

17

Shape hood using existing creases.

The creases at the front and back of the robe, should be very sharp to ensure robe does not open outward too far.

Martial arts figure

Martial arts figure

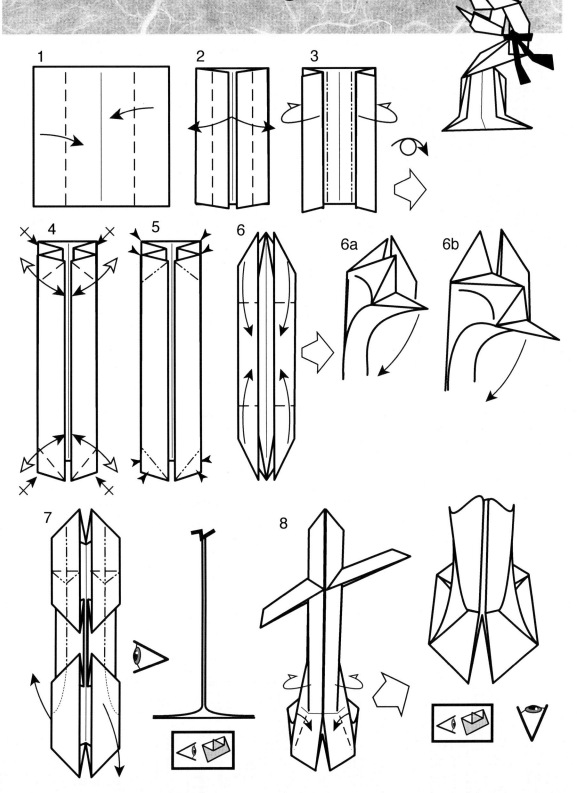

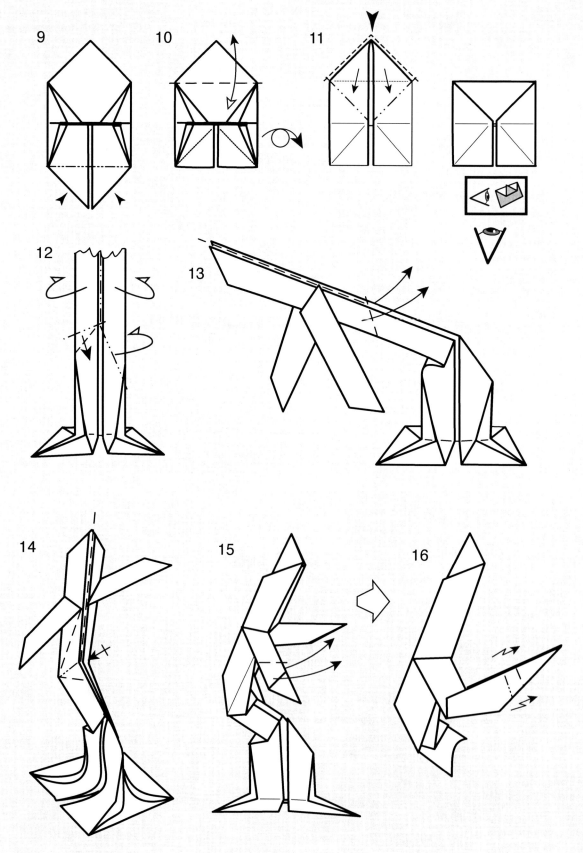

9

10

11

12

13

14

15

16

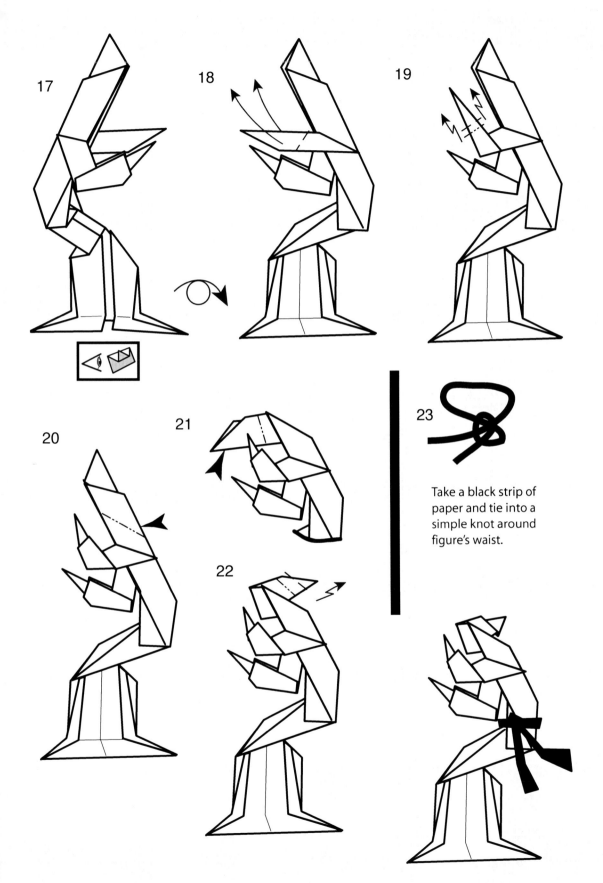

17

18

19

20

21

22

23

Take a black strip of paper and tie into a simple knot around figure's waist.

Cool werewolf

Cool werewolf

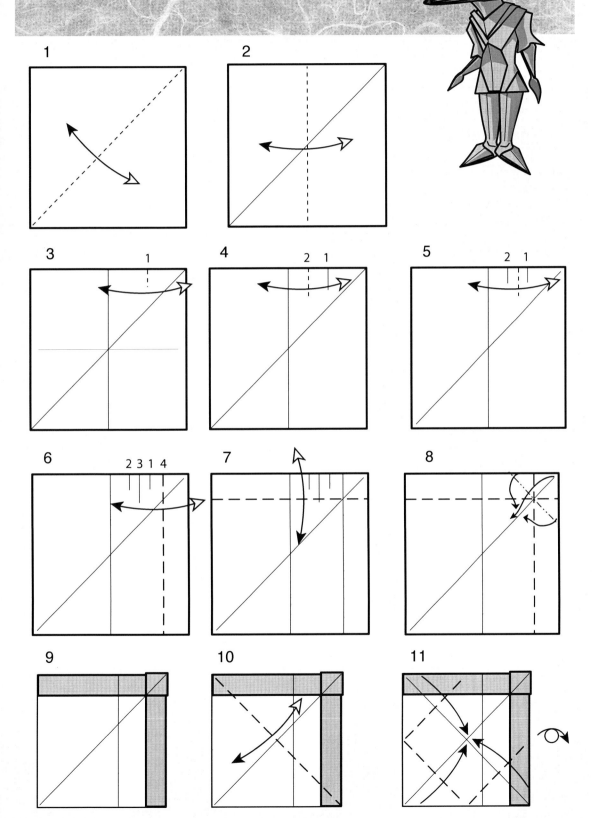

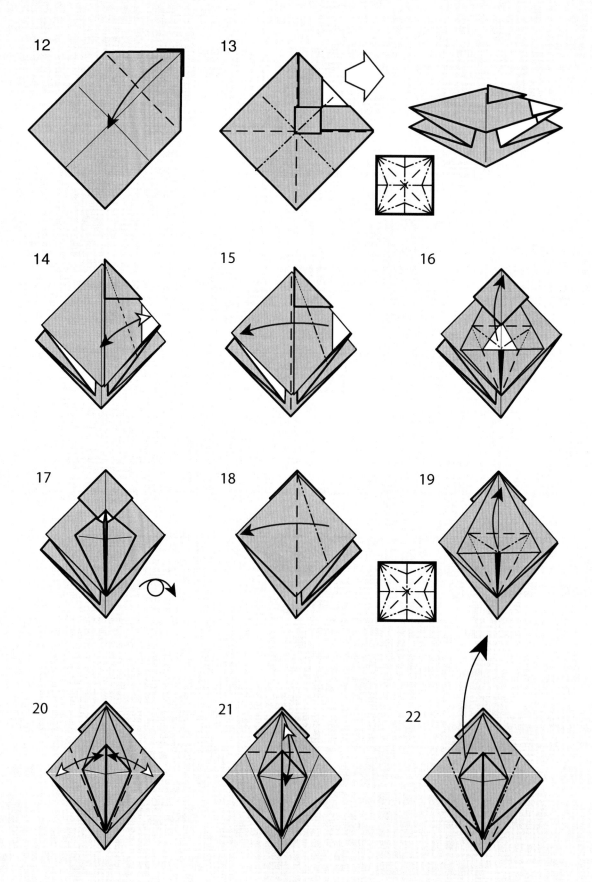

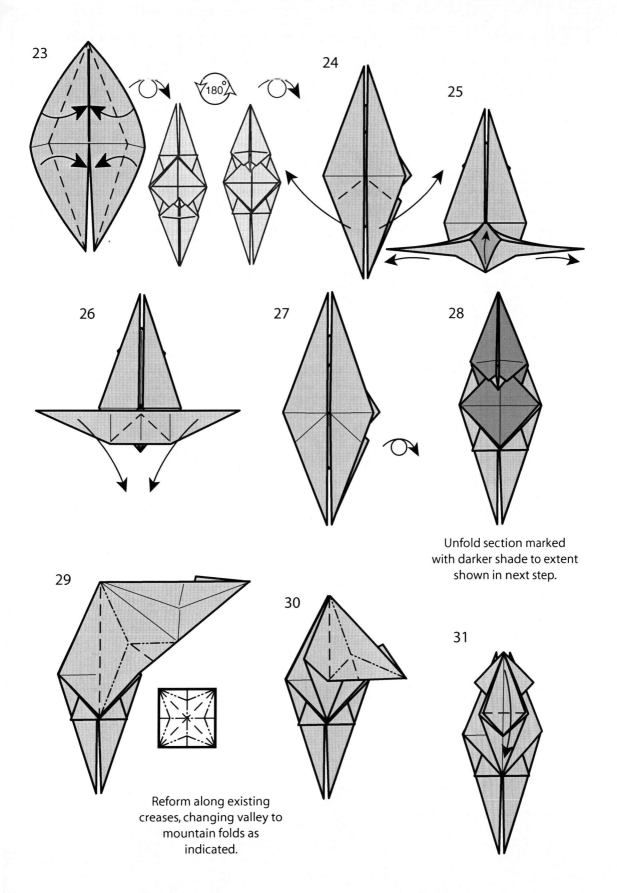

23

24

25

26

27

28

Unfold section marked
with darker shade to extent
shown in next step.

29

Reform along existing
creases, changing valley to
mountain folds as
indicated.

30

31

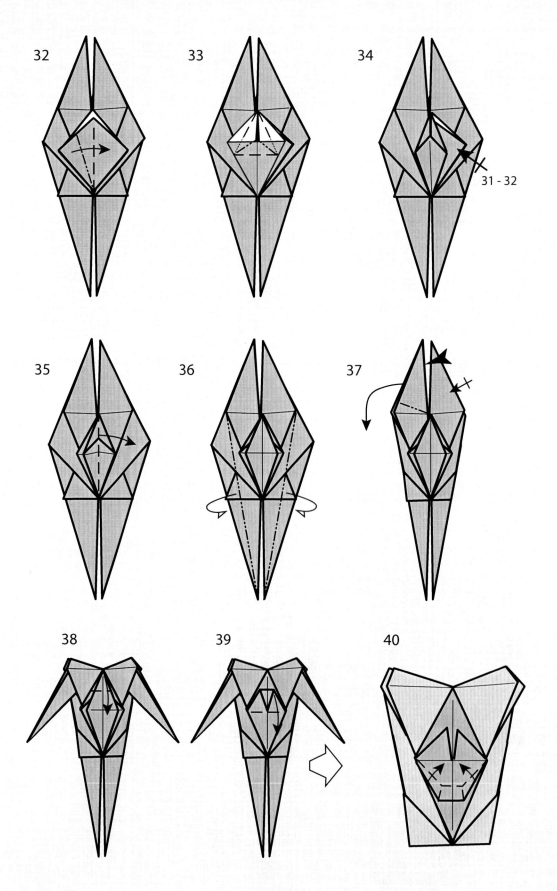

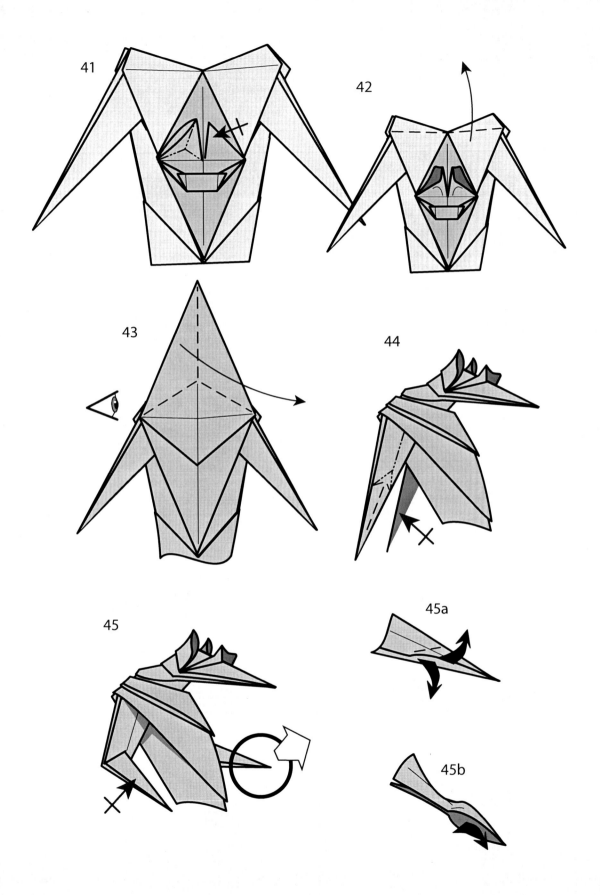

41

42

43

44

45

45a

45b

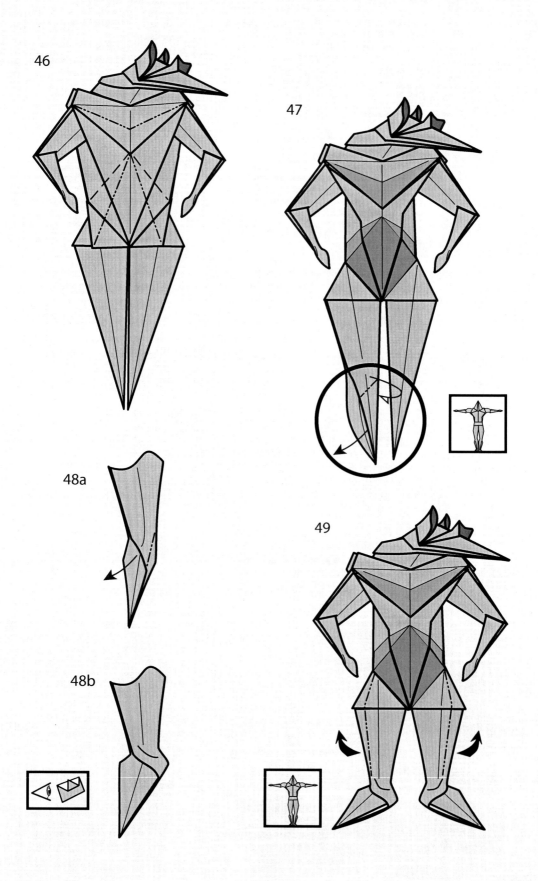

46

47

48a

48b

49

50

51

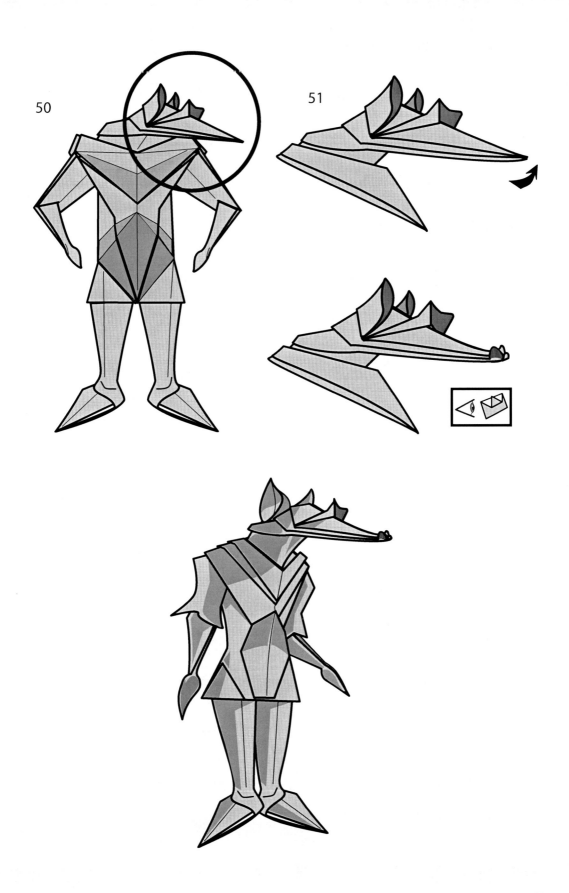

The werewolf can be made without the 'cool' sunglasses by using the following alternative folds for the eyes. Replace the numbered steps with those shown below.

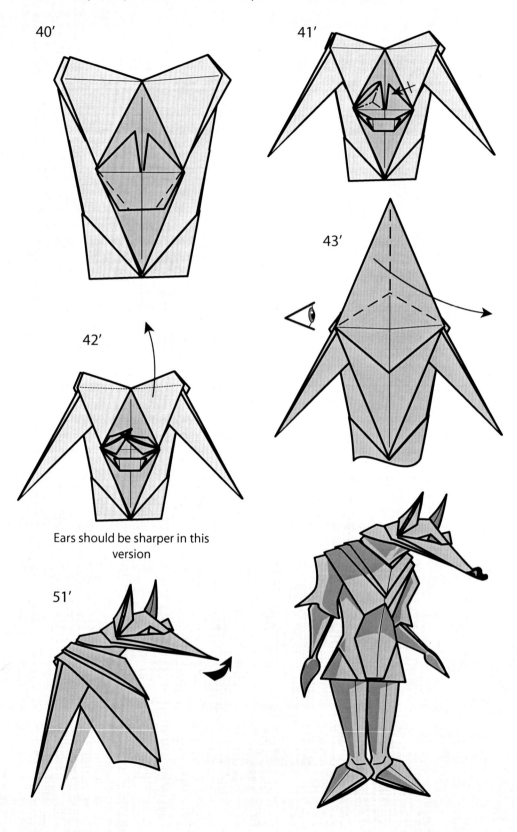

40′

41′

43′

42′

Ears should be sharper in this version

51′

Origami Ninjas

Ninja jumping frogs

[Kanji characters state: 'Ninja Frog']

Ninja jumping frog

Download Ninja Frog papers from
www.sorceryoforigami.co.uk

1

2

3

4

5

6

7

8

9

10

11

12

13

14

15

16

17

13 - 16

18

Press here with a finger to make it jump.

Ninja

Ninja

1

Paper - black
both sides
recommended.

2

3

4

5

6

7

8

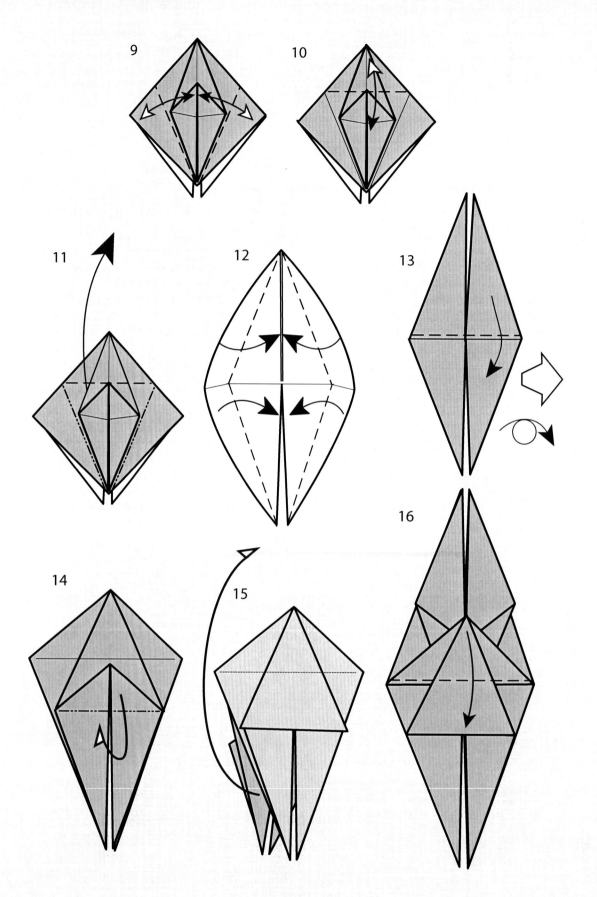

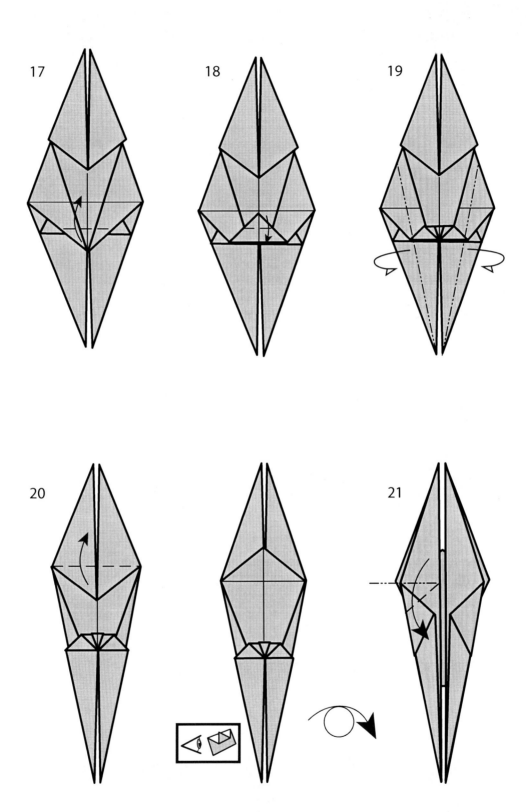

17

18

19

20

21

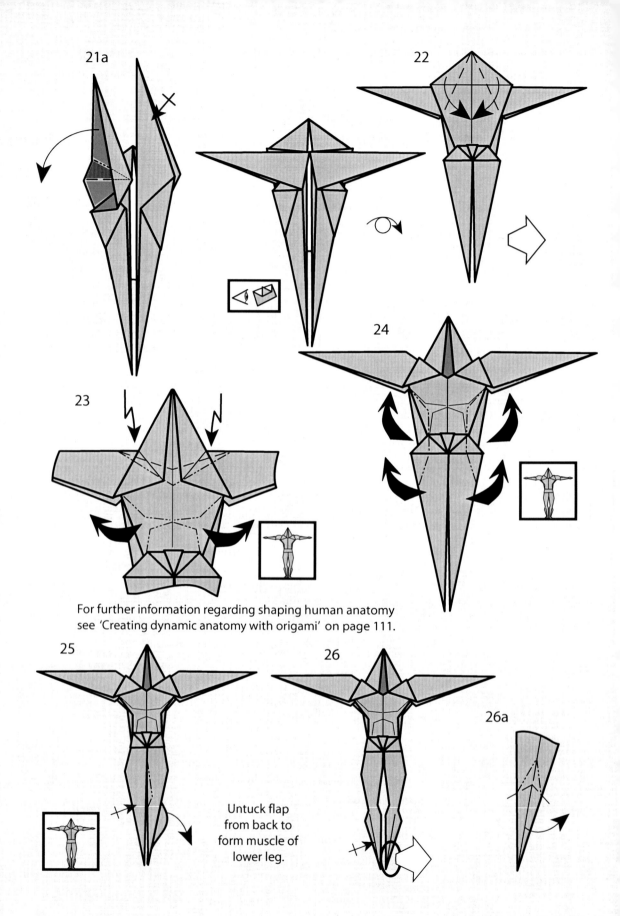

21a

22

23

24

For further information regarding shaping human anatomy see 'Creating dynamic anatomy with origami' on page 111.

25

26

26a

Untuck flap from back to form muscle of lower leg.

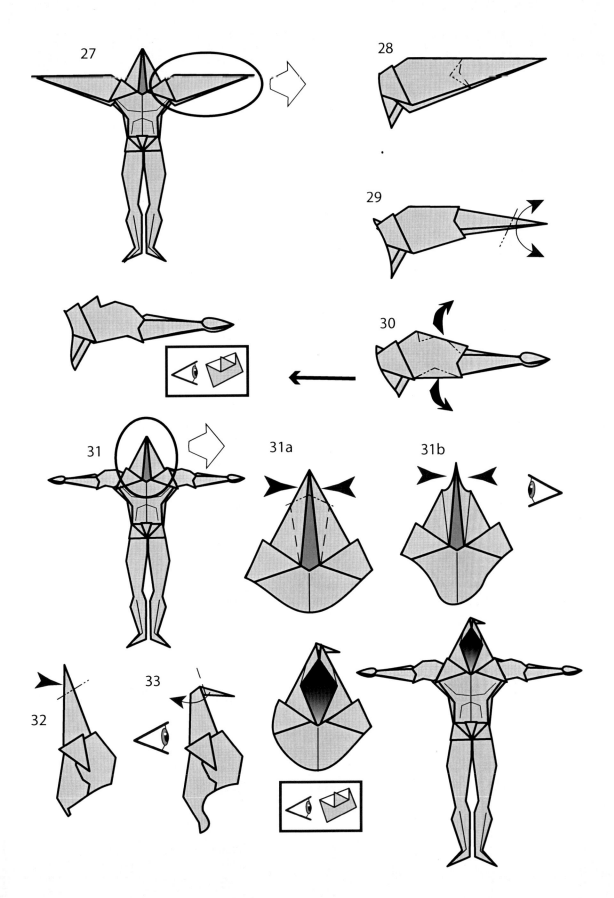

Ninja belt

1

2

3

4

5

6

Tie in a knot

Try other colour combinations of Ninja and
belt - white Ninja red belt, etc.

Katana (Ninja sword)

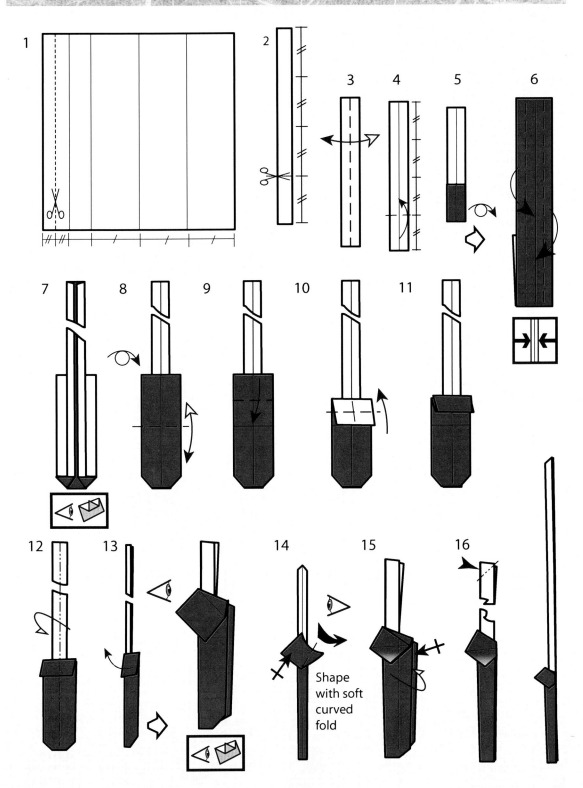

Shape
with soft
curved
fold

Nunchukas

Thanks to Jo Goh for modelling this shot. [Kanji characters state: 'Ninja']

Nunchakas

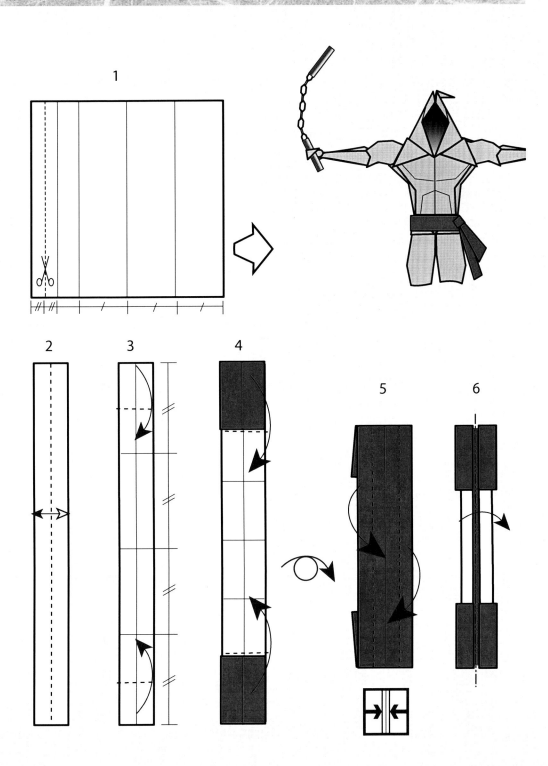

1

2

3

4

5

6

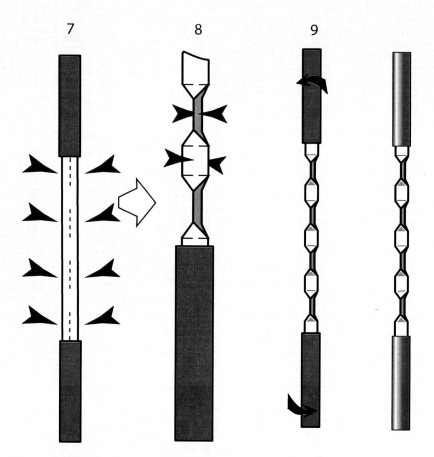

7 **8** **9**

The chain links are simulated by squashing the white section of the paper at regular intervals at 90° to each other.

Secure weapon in hand with Blu-Tack or similar adhesive, or glue dot.

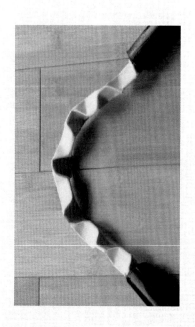

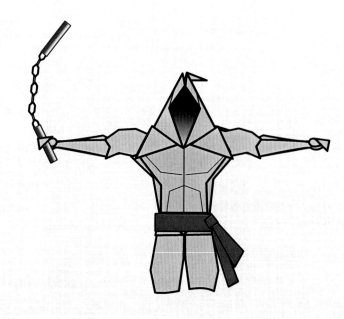

Shuriken* (Ninja throwing star)
Traditional model
*sword hidden in user's hand

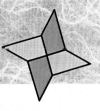

1

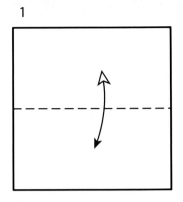

2

3

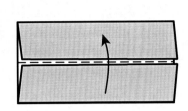

Make 2 of these.

A4

B4

Note: A has open side to top and B to bottom.

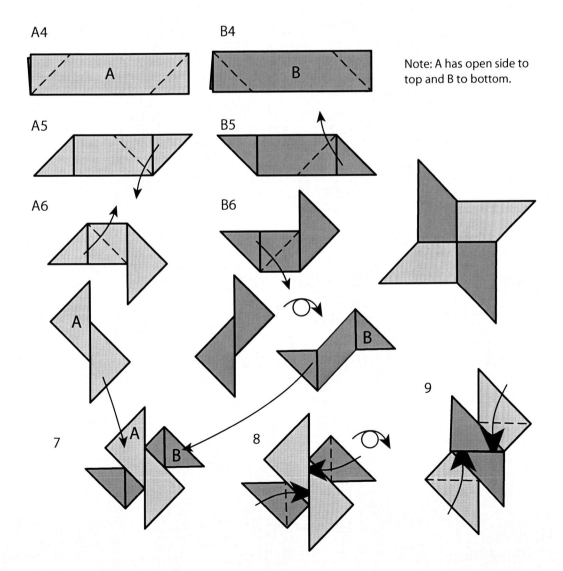

A5

B5

A6

B6

A

B

7

8

9

101

Elita Ninja

Elite Ninja body

Follow the instructions for the Ninja, (page 91), and at step 31 follow the instructions below.

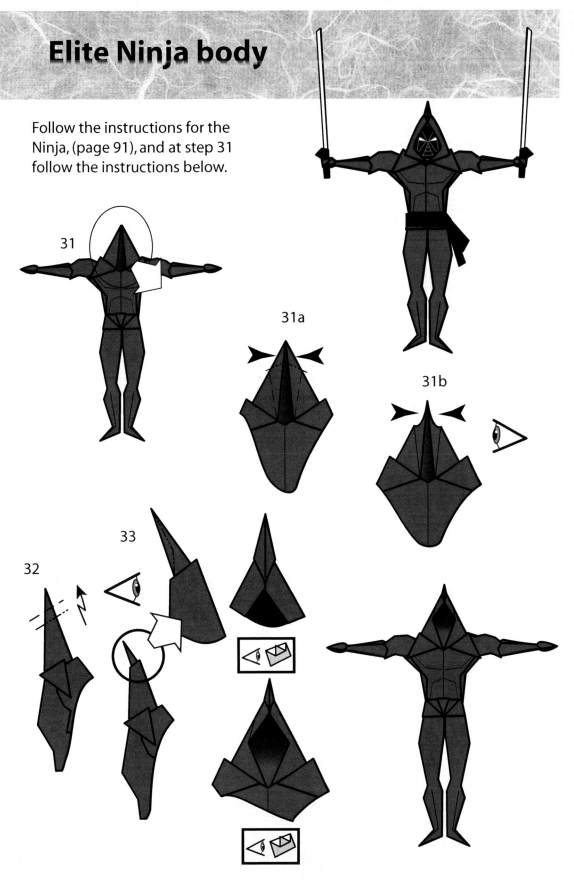

31

31a

31b

32

33

Elite Ninja mask

First make the body (previous page) using the Elite Ninja diagrams. The mask is a separate piece of paper.

Use the adjacent size guide to determine the size of paper for the mask.

In proportion - size of paper used for ninja body

Mask is 3½ times smaller than the height of the paper for the body.

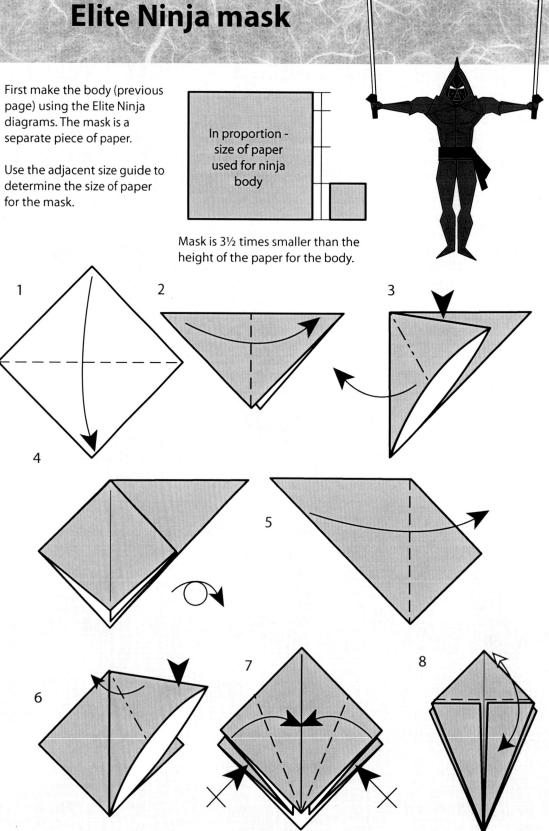

1

2

3

4

5

6

7

8

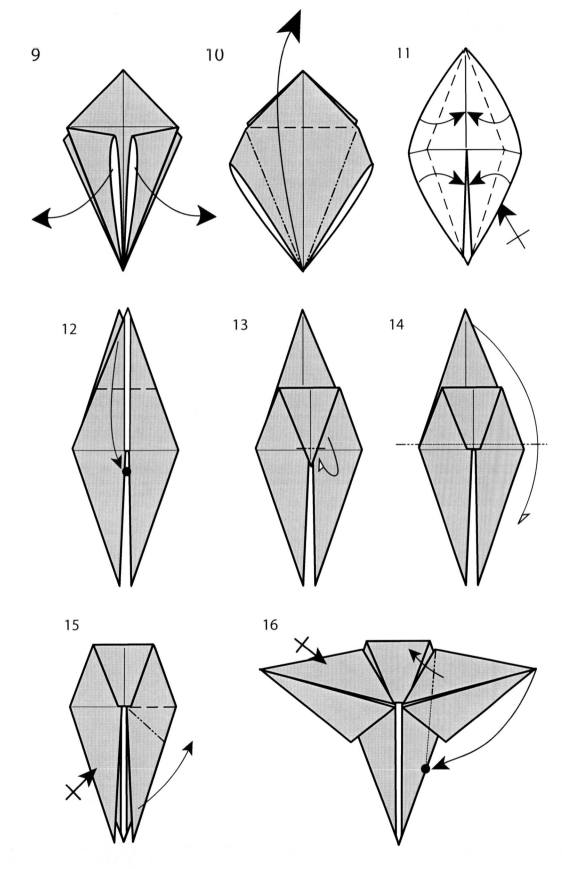

17

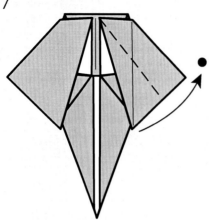

18

a

b

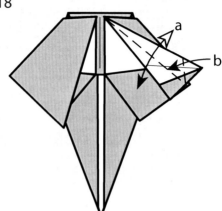

19

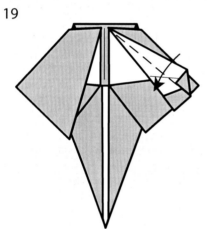

20

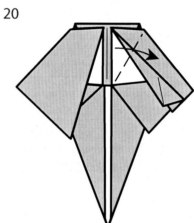

21

17 - 20

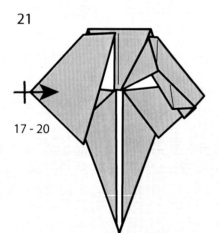

22

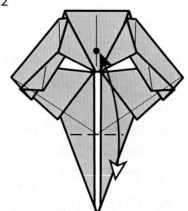

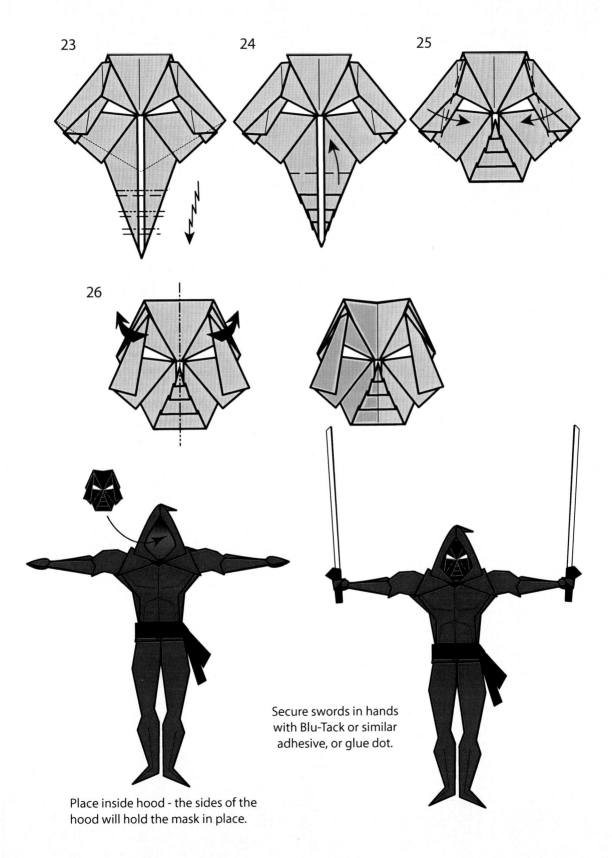

23

24

25

26

Place inside hood - the sides of the hood will hold the mask in place.

Secure swords in hands with Blu-Tack or similar adhesive, or glue dot.

Sky Ninja

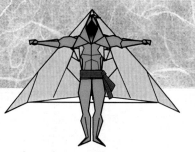

Make a Ninja (page 91), following the instructions for the Origami Ninja model, except make in light blue. Then make the sky-blade below.

Sky Blade - Ninja glider

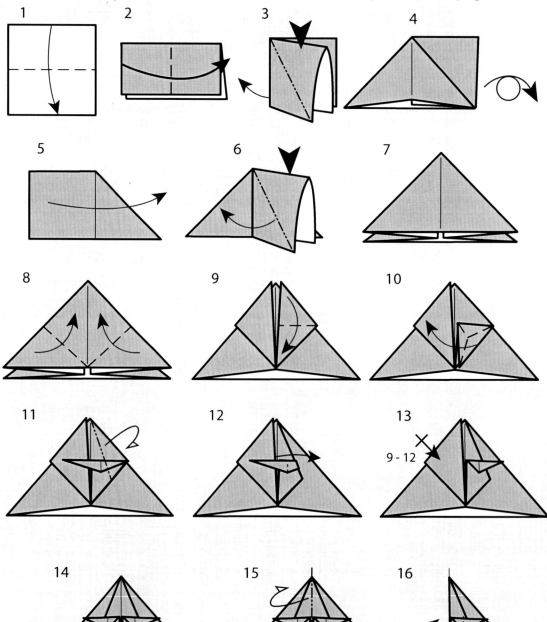

1

2

3

4

5

6

7

8

9

10

11

12

13

9 - 12

14

15

16

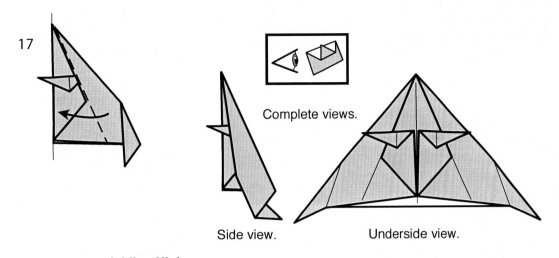

17

Complete views.

Side view.

Underside view.

Adding Ninja

18

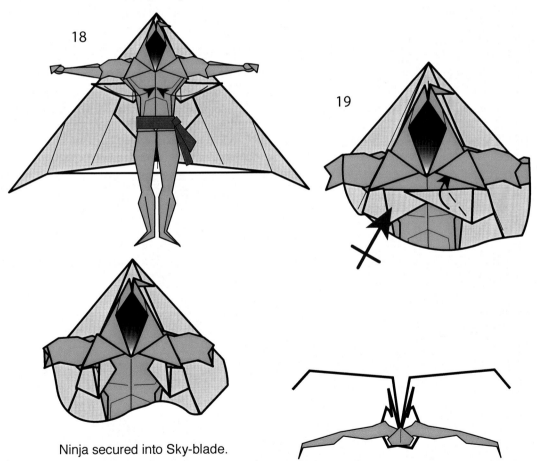

19

Ninja secured into Sky-blade.

Top view showing how wings and figure should be arranged when flying.

Stand for figures

Suitable for Ninja models. Use same size paper as figure.

1

2

3

4

5

6

7

8

Line up with layer below.

9

10

11

12

Tuck in pocket.

10 - 11

13

14a

14

After this fold the stand will not lay flat.

15

16

Place tip of stand in pocket at rear of figure under shoulder blades.

Creating dynamic anatomy with origami

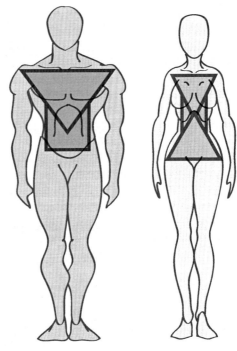

At the end of the folding sequence for some of the figures in this book, the diagrams suggest sculpting the features of human anatomy. For the best results, an understanding of human anatomy will assist you in achieving more realistic results than by merely replicating the fold lines in the diagrams. This guide is an attempt to show more clearly how a heroic figure can be achieved with photographic references.

There are two essential steps to understanding the application of human anatomy to origami.
1. human proportions.
2. body shapes and muscle forms.

1. human proportions

There are many books depicting human anatomy, but to study the subject deeply is a daunting prospect. However, for our purposes, we do not need to know the precise details and Latin names of muscles and tendons. We only need to know the basic proportions of various parts of the body in relation to one another. Figure 1 shows the relationship of various parts of the body comparing lengths. The figure also shows a simplification of muscle forms of the male figure.

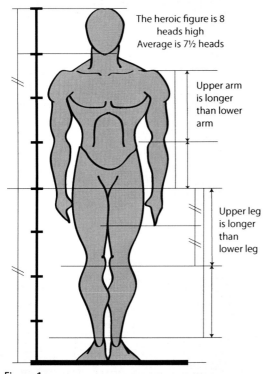

The heroic figure is 8 heads high
Average is 7½ heads

Upper arm is longer than lower arm

Upper leg is longer than lower leg

Figure 1

Figure 2

2. body shapes and muscle forms

Origami leads itself to representing subjects in a simplified form – reducing the essential elements to basic shapes. There is a basic difference between the male and female figures. Understanding this difference is essential to clearly differentiate whether our figure is male of female. Women generally have hips that are as wide or wider than their shoulders while the opposite is true for males. This basic difference is evident even in the human skeleton. Women have a much broader pelvic bone and narrower shoulder width than men.

In Figure 2 we can see the torso reduced to very basic shapes. We can represent the male figure with a triangle pointing down and a rectangle underneath. The female figure is the opposite. In the female's case the triangle is pointing upward with the rectangle on top. The narrowness of the shoulders is represented by the second smaller triangle at the top. We can exploit this in our figures, and provide instant recognition of the male or female form.

In respect of arms, legs and head, the male is more muscular and angular. This can be rendered in origami by the use of bulkier angular folds, whereas in a female, while still having the same muscular shapes for the arms and legs, the forms are less prominent with softer gentle curves. Therefore, by understanding this simple principle, we can make our origami figure represent male of female forms.

The following steps indicate how to sculpt the male anatomy using the hybrid bird-frog base used for the ninja in this book.

The photograph above shows the figure base unfolded to reveal all the creases which form the anatomy shaping.

Chest

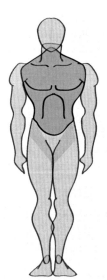

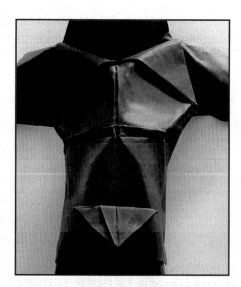

The mountain folds of the chest curve around the body. The first step is to consider the need to represent the male torso shape (downward facing triangle as discussed earlier and illustrated in figure 2).

The abdominal muscles are spilt in to eight segments on the well developed heroic figure (commonly inaccurately named 'six pack'). However we are simplifying this by outlining the entire area with an arch shape of valley folds.

On the male figure the hips are only slightly wider than the waist.

Head/hood

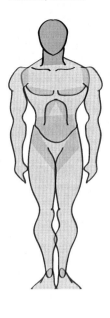

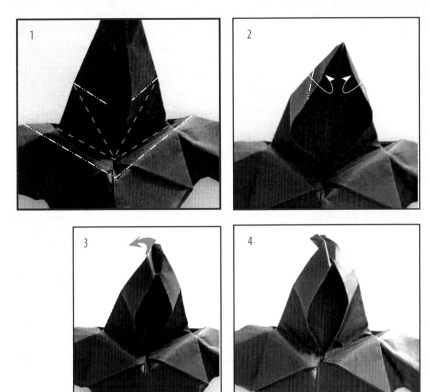

The collar bone has been shaped by the zig zag folds shown in the chest section. The hood is shaped by two valley and mountain folds which open up the hood. The hood is locked into place by an inside reverse fold at the top of the hood (photo 2), the resultant tab is then bent slightly to one side.

Figures Left arm

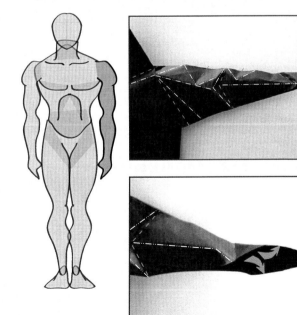

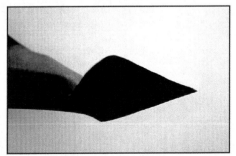

For the arms , the length of the upper and lower arms shoulder to elbow and elbow to wrist are important to establish first. See figure 1 (page 111) for a guide. Mark these lengths with a simple crease. Similarly mark the length of the hand.

Figures Right arm

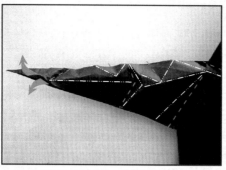

The muscles are then shaped as shown.

The hand is formed by untucking paper from the back of the layer underneath.

Figures Right leg

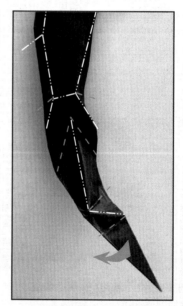

Like the arms, the first step for the legs is to decide upon the lengths of the divisions of the upper and lower leg (hip to knee, knee to ankle, and the length of the foot). See figure 1 for a guide. Mark these lengths with a simple crease.

The muscle forms are then shaped as shown.

Figures Left leg

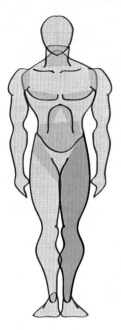   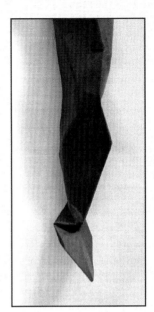

Repeat for the left leg.

An understanding of human anatomy will be of great benefit to create more realistic origami figures. The better your understanding, the more intuitive your origami shaping of the human form will be.

Next...